I Did It My Ways

I Did It
My Ways

A memoir by

D'yan Forest

with **Stephen Clarke**

An 86-year-old stand-up comedian's
lifelong journey from prudish Bostonian to
scandalous *Parisienne*, and beyond...

pAf

D'yan Forest is a comedian, singer, pianist and ukulele player who has been performing professionally for more than 50 years. Her shows have included *A Broad Abroad* (which she took to the Edinburgh Festival), *I Married a Nun*, *My Pussy Is Purring Again*, and most recently *Swinging on the Seine*, the story of her outrageous exploits in the sex parties, strip clubs and transvestite cabarets of Paris, which she has performed in France and the USA. She lives in New York City, the Hamptons and Paris.

Stephen Clarke is a British writer living in Paris. He has written six novels with *Merde* in the title, including *A Year in the Merde* (a worldwide bestseller in more than 20 languages) and *Merde Actually* (number one in the UK). His history books include *1,000 Years of Annoying the French* (a number-one bestseller in the UK) and *How the French Won Waterloo, Or Think They Did*. He has also written a stage version of his novel *The Merde Factor*, as well as a radio sitcom, jokes and songs. He co-wrote D'yan Forest's show *Swinging on the Seine*. He occasionally performs his comedy songs in clubs, for fun (his own rather than the audience's).

Disclaimer:

All opinions are my own.
I also made up some of the facts.
But hell, this is memoir, not history.
—D'yan Forest, 2021

Contents

Introduction

I'M 86 YEARS OLD, AND AT DIFFERENT TIMES IN MY LIFE I'VE been Diana Ruth Shulman, Diana Lunn Shulman, Diana Lunn, Mrs. Irwin Cohen, Dee Dee Bumps and D'yan Forest. I've been so many people.

At college, I was the only Jew in the Christian choir. When I was a Boston housewife, I was the only woman who took her husband vacationing on gay beaches. When I was a nightclub singer in New York, I was the only American pretending to be French (mainly because my Jewish agent said I looked too Jewish). At Paris swingers' parties, I was the only person yearning for a bit of romanticism during the orgy.

And these days, I'm always the oldest comedian in the club, usually by about 50 years.

I've lived a life, as the famous song says, that's full. And I've always done things my way. Or rather, my *ways*.

Sometimes it worked out for the best, and occasionally it all went terribly wrong.

So regrets, I've had a few. But I've also enjoyed myself in ways that most people wouldn't even dare to try.

And that's what this memoir is all about.

Chapter 1

The Famously Jewish City of Boston

I'M A PERFORMER, A REBEL, A SWIMMER AND GOLFER, AND JEWISH. That much I know. And I was all of those things almost as soon as I was born. Except for the golf, of course.

Things started to get complicated very early on.

I arrived on 31 July, 1934 in Boston, Massachusetts. And I was almost born in the middle of a lake.

My parents were vacationing in a camp resort twenty miles outside of town. Not that we were actually camping. My mother would never go anywhere that didn't have an indoor bathroom. So, this was a luxury type of place, a huddle of log cabins set in shady woodland, by a large greenish lake. It looked a lot like an old trappers' settlement, except for the huge Fords and Dodges parked outside all the cabins, and the loud female voices calling out across the woodland: "Hey, Marge, you get me those herrings at the market?" Yes, this was a *Jewish* camp resort. Back then in America, land of the free, Jews had to go on vacation with Jews. The WASPs wanted to keep their nests for themselves.

When my mother wasn't cooking or yelling at my father, she was in the lake. And on this July day, she decided to go for her usual morning swim, even though she was hugely pregnant.

Dad had already fetched the morning paper—he was a lawyer and liked to keep up with who was suing whom in Boston. My brother, Herbie, was ten, so he just gobbled down some toast and ran off to play with his friends at being Jewish Apaches. And Mom heaved herself up from the breakfast table and said: "I'm going for a swim."

Dad knew there was no point arguing. He'd already said it would be better to go back to town to be near the hospital. He'd already said my mother ought to lie down and rest. But Mom, the judge in our family court, had ignored his summing-up, and continued to cook, hobble over to the next cabin to talk to the neighbors, and swim.

"Don't try and stop me," she told Dad, who wasn't trying to stop her. "I can't hear you anyway, I've taken out my hearing aid." She was very deaf, and had already waterlogged one hearing aid during this vacation, so she was being really careful with the spare one. "I'm going for a swim."

"Don't dive in or you'll empty the lake," Dad said, smiling to himself. He loved to joke, even when no one was really listening. Or when they'd taken out their hearing aid.

"What did you say?" my mother asked. "But it doesn't matter. I'm going for a swim."

So, pulling on her bathing cap that made her look like a human daisy (with, in the ninth month of her pregnancy, an especially bloated stem), she waddled down to the lake-side, dropped her bathrobe on to a picnic table where some people were trying to have breakfast, and waddled across the little sandy beach into the water.

Maybe it was the warm summer lake that made her body think she was in one of those modern birthing tanks. But she'd only gone about three strokes out from the beach when she suddenly started yelling even louder than usual.

"Louie!"

Dad looked up from his paper (as did all the other adult cabin dwellers on the campsite—Mom could have yelled for the Olympics).

"Loooouuuiieeee! It's coming! The baby's coming! It's coming out right now!"

Dad rushed to the lake, wondering how long a baby could survive under water.

As usual, Mom was exaggerating slightly. It was just the first labor pain. She crawled out of the lake, and, still in her swimsuit, lay down in the back of our huge Ford. Dad drove her to the Boston Lying In Hospital, while she continued to scream with every labor pain: "It's coming out! Right now!"

She held on till they got to the hospital. And for several hours after that: "The baby's coming out! Right now! This time it really is!"

I finally emerged around 3 am on 1 July 1934 into a perfectly dry maternity ward. But I was *almost* born in the middle of a lake. That's probably why I go swimming pretty much every day of my life, even when I'm traveling around the world. I always search out the nearest pool or lake. I'm what you could call a water baby. Or maybe some kind of human herring.

* * *

MY FAMILY WAS LIVING IN Roxbury, Massachusetts, where the
first generation of Jewish immigrants moved when they could
afford to get out of Boston. It was a genteel, mainly Gentile,
middle-class neighborhood, with a mix of family houses and
low-rise apartments. Roxbury was a fine place to live, but for
some reason my parents decided that they wanted to move
up even more in the world. This was before the nuclear age,
but maybe they decided that as a two-kid nuclear family, we
had to become truly American. So my Grandpa, who had
money, bought us a house in Newton, a suburb in the west
of Boston that had big houses with lawns and backyards, the
kind of place a lawyer should live.

My father was a family lawyer, dealing in real estate, divorce, wills and accidents, and giving out as much free advice
to friends and neighbors as he did to his clients. People
would call in the middle of the night, and he would patiently
talk them through their problem. It used to drive Mom nuts:
"You gave him a hundred dollars' worth of legal advice for
free—at midnight? You'll bankrupt us!"

Dad would tell us all the details of his supposedly secret
cases at the dinner table, and I was so fascinated that I said I
wanted to be a lawyer like him. I imagined he'd be delighted,
but he ordered me, no, don't do it, or you'll never find a husband. I'm sure he gave his male friends better advice than that.

Then there was my brother Herbie, and my mother, who
didn't work, was partially deaf and went crazy from time to

time. Anything could set her off. Like, once I said I didn't like the grilled cheese she'd cooked, so she picked up the cheese and threw it at the wall and started yelling "What's wrong with my cheese? You're never satisfied! I spend hours in the kitchen and all you do is wolf it down if you like it or throw it at me if you don't! You're all the same! You hate me!" And so on, until the windows started rattling. You've heard of opera singers who can crack a wine glass? Mom's voice would have smashed the bottle.

While she was shrieking, Dad would always stay as calm as a polar bear in a snowstorm. He would grab my hand and take me out for a walk around the neighborhood. There was a park nearby, and to distract me from the chaos at home, he would say we were going to see something really exciting at the park. When we got there, he'd say, "Look, see that squirrel up that tree?" Well, there was a squirrel in just about every tree in Newton, but he'd say this squirrel was the national tree-climbing champion, and it was going to the squirrel Olympic Games. And when he finished joking around, he'd assure me quietly that Mom's mood would blow over, so there was no need to worry. And if it was summer, he'd take me to the drugstore to buy a college ice—vanilla ice cream, chocolate syrup, nuts and marshmallow—and the druggist would know what was going on, and he'd tell Dad, "don't worry, Dolly's going through that difficult time of life." Everybody in the neighborhood knew about Mom, and called her Dolly, instead of her given name, Dorothy. They liked her because when she was wasn't yelling and throwing things, she was one of the kindest, most generous women you could meet. For instance, a guy called Mr. Turpin would come over and mow the lawn and do odd jobs, and Mom would give him clothes for his kids, and chat about his family.

When we finally went back home with the ice cream, she was usually upstairs in bed sleeping, and by the next day, or maybe the day after, she would wake up, and be back to her old self and not remember a thing.

Dad knew exactly how to deal with Mom. For example, I remember he used to smoke cigars. They helped him to relax while he was looking over legal papers or reading the newspaper. But one day Mom burst into the living room and went nuts: "Why do you have to stink my house up? You want the curtains to smell like a pool hall in Havana?"

Dad didn't bother to argue. Next day, he came home with a pipe. He puffed on it, swanking around in front of the mirror in the hall, looking very distinguished, like some university professor. Even Mom laughed. Though of course she still complained about the smoke in the living room.

Then after a week or so of pipe-smoking, Dad said he'd developed a pain in his jaw. Mom seized the opportunity: "It's all that tobacco smoke! It's rotting your face!" She knew about the dangers of smoke decades before anyone else. She made him promise to go to the family doctor.

He went to see Doctor Salz, a cousin of my mother's, but when Dad came home, he said the Doc hadn't been able to find a cause for the pain.

"Go to the dentist then!" Mom ordered him. So, he made an appointment with the dentist, but when he came home, he said the dentist had told him his gums and teeth were fine.

"Go to a specialist!" Mom said.

"What kind of specialist?" Dad asked. "A faceologist? A cheekiatrist?" He winked at me as he said it.

"A brain surgeon!" Mom said. "You need your whole head examined!"

So, Dad found some kind of head doctor at the hospital, and went along, and this time he came home with good news.

"The specialist diagnosed the problem," he announced triumphantly.

"Too much tobacco," Mom said.

"No. It's a common condition called jawcrampitis," Dad said, winking at me again. "I've been gripping the pipe too tight with my teeth."

"So, you have to stop smoking the pipe," Mom said, delighted.

"Yes," he confirmed, giving me another discreet wink. "But to avoid nervous exhaustion from suddenly giving up tobacco, I have to start smoking cigars again. They're much softer on the jaw muscles."

Mom started to boil over, but Dad calmed her down. "Honey, it was the specialist who told me to do it. You were the one who told me to go and consult him, right?"

And he was back on the cigars, and Mom was back to yelling at him about living in a Havana pool hall. Dad thought he'd won a victory, but Mom put her foot down, and from then on, he could only smoke in the den. No more smelly curtains.

* * *

MOM'S MOODS DIDN'T ALWAYS END in a negotiated settlement. Once she punched me in the face and gave me a black eye.

I was 16 years old and was going to a Valentine's dance that evening at the temple. It was going to be my first ever Valentine's dance. I was all excited, and I was chatting to a girlfriend on the phone about what to wear.

"Should I wear a real ball gown? I'd love to, but it's so hard to dance in a ball gown. And mine is a bit low-cut for the temple. Too daring. Or is it? What do you think?"

We were chatting away, wondering what the boys would think of our dresses, wondering what the other girls would say, when my mother burst in the room.

"Get off the phone Diana! You've been on there for hours!"

I should have turned around and looked at her. I would have seen she was in one of her screaming moods. But all I did was turn away even further, so I could hear what my friend was saying, while I waved a hand at Mom: "Shhh!"

Next thing I knew, her fist was smacking into my face, practically knocking me out. I just managed to say goodbye before I dropped the phone. My eye was already swelling up and my nose was bleeding. I stood there, trembling with shock and pain, and looking into my mother's horrified eyes. She saw what she'd done, and regretted it instantly, but it was done. About three hours before my first big teenage dance, and I looked like a boxer who'd lost ten rounds in a row.

Mom took me into her room and sat me down in front of her mirror. While I held a wad of cotton to my bleeding nose, she dabbed foundation and powder around my eye, which was getting bigger and redder by the minute. She even gave the other eye some extra mascara and dark eye shadow to try and even up the colors. But it didn't do much good. By the time I got to the dance, my face was swollen and thickly pasted with make-up. Now I just looked like someone who was trying to hide the fact they'd been punched in the face.

"Oh my God, what happened!" my girlfriends asked me. I gave them the reply that Mom told me to try.

"I walked into a doorknob."

It would have meant that I had been walking on my knees, but my girlfriends seemed to believe me.

As for the boys, they didn't care. Not one of them came to speak to me. I spent the whole evening sitting out every dance. I guess the boys thought I might start a brawl if they stepped on my toes during a waltz.

Next day, we left to go skiing in North Conway, New Hampshire for the February vacation. By now my swollen eye had reached its full size, as if someone had glued half a plum on my face. I didn't know what hurt more—my bruised eye socket or my pride. My Valentine's dance had been ruined, and now the vacation was going to be a social disaster, too. I was pretty shy at the time, but with my boxer-in-make-up face, I was practically a recluse.

We went to the one inn at the ski resort that allowed Jews to stay, and my parents mixed with their friends from Boston, while I kept to myself. There was an older man at the inn, also from Boston, who took an interest in me, and I ended up telling him the true story of the black eye. I poured out my heart to him.

"I'm never going to date a boy. I'll never be popular. I'll just be the girl who walks into knee-high doorknobs."

This older man was very sympathetic.

"Don't talk nonsense, Diana. As soon as the swelling goes down, you'll have lots of dates. You'll look great. In fact, if it's not a bad joke, you look pretty *swell* now."

I was really grateful to him for cheering me up like that, and for listening to this little, lonely 16-year-old girl. A couple of months later I decided to look for his phone number and call him up. A woman answered the phone, and when he came on the line, I was disappointed because he didn't seem to want to talk like we had done at the ski resort. We had a very short conversation and then he hung up.

Innocence, innocence.

NEWTON WAS A PRETTY CHIC neighborhood. It had a country club and a golf club, and one of the best school systems in the United States. What it didn't have was Jews.

Not that we were very Jewish. We didn't go to synagogue that often, except three days a year during the high Jewish holidays. I know there are a lot of Jewish mother jokes around, but I don't have any because my mother was desperate to be a WASP. We even used to put up a Christmas tree.

I remember our first-ever Christmas tree. I was about five years old when I saw that our Catholic neighbors had a tree in their living room, and their kids were decorating it with candles and streamers.

I went home and asked Mom if we could have one, too.

"No, we don't put up Christmas trees," she said. "Christmas is a Christian festival. The clue is in the name." Or something like that. Mom wanted to look like a WASP, but she didn't want to *be* one. It was such a final "no" that I started crying. And didn't stop. All the rest of that day and night, I cried at the injustice of the world. Why couldn't Jews have Christmas trees? It didn't seem fair.

In the end, of course it was Dad who decided to end this particular injustice.

He convinced Mom that it would be good to fit in with the rest of the neighborhood—the WASP side, anyway.

"I can go and get the whole Christmas kit in one go from Morris's Discount Christmas Outlet," he said. This was a big Boston store with the slogan: "Catering to Conflicted Jews throughout Greater New England." Dad had other Jewish friends who went there and stocked up on everything that a house needed to look WASPy or Catholic in December.

Mom wasn't so sure.

"But what if our Jewish neighbors see you driving home with a Christmas tree?" she wailed. "What if the *rabbi* sees you?"

"Don't worry," Dad reassured her. "A friend of mine told me what to do."

I waited excitedly as Dad drove off, and watched out the window for his return. And when he came back a couple of hours later, and drove straight into the garage, I almost started crying again. There was no Christmas tree poking out the window or the trunk.

I ran through the kitchen into the garage, and all I could see of Dad were his legs, poking out from below the rear fender.

I thought he had managed to run himself over, and really did start to cry. Then he emerged, smiling, pulling with him the trunk and lower branches of a Christmas tree.

He'd been so scared that other Jews would see him bringing the tree home that he tied it underneath the car.

Every year after that we had a tree and stockings, and the whole Christmas thing. Once, when my more religious grandfather came over, we had to hide the Christmas tree in the attic while Mom kept him busy eating a big piece of apple cake that she'd made for Hanukkah, but other than that, around the end of December, we behaved pretty much like all the Catholic and WASP families in the neighborhood. Except for singing the carols, of course. There was no way we were going to start singing "Onward Christian Soldiers"—not yet, anyway. That's a story I'll tell later, when I get to college.

ANOTHER WASP-STYLE THING DAD DID—for his own pleasure, not mine—was play golf. This was pretty difficult for Jewish people in the 1930s, because almost all the private clubs didn't let Jews join. (Sports weren't too important when Washington and Co. were putting together the Constitution, which must explain why they didn't think to extend equal rights to the golf course.)

To show you how tough it was, some Jewish people from our neighborhood used to drive to another suburb where there was a 14-hole public course. Yes, 14. This was not some kind of Jewish ritual number. Apparently, a full-size 18-hole course had been planned, but some local residents opposed the building of the course, so they ended up with only 14 holes, and had to calculate their scores and handicaps by doing some very complex mathematics. You'd have thought it would have been simpler just to let people of all religious beliefs join all the golf clubs.

But a lot of Jewish men were keen on golf in Boston in the 30s. This was because, like my father, they had been newsboys as kids, and the WASPs used to take the newsboys out to their resort at Lake Charlton, New Hampshire, to act as caddies at the weekend. And on the Monday, the boys were allowed to play.

So Dad picked up golf as a boy, and carried on playing golf as an adult. This was also why my brother Herbie and I started playing when we were young, long before the sport became really popular in the USA. Mom played as well, and in the summer, when I came home from camp, we used to go out to the New England Inn, and I would caddy for my parents. I learned about golf the same way as my father, except I didn't have to deliver the newspapers first.

BEING JEWISH IN NEWTON COULD get lonely. I remember that there was only one other Jewish student in my whole grade school, and she and I didn't have too many friends. At first there was another Jewish family on our street, but they moved away when the husband committed suicide in a nearby pond (I never knew why). Anyway, I grew up thinking that the world was a non-Jewish kind of place.

Some people in the neighborhood wanted it to stay that way. Once, when Dad was washing the car on the street on a Sunday, the police came and told him to stop. Someone had called the cops because he was working on a Sunday, and that was against the law in Catholic Boston.

This is not to say that our neighbors weren't friendly. Mister Murphy next door was the Head Gardener for Boston College, so we got into the football games for free. When I was ten years old, his son Junie Murphy came home from the war, during which he had played in a Navy band. And he started to teach me the trumpet.

Ah yes, the war....

Chapter 2

World War Two: Not a Great Time to Be Jewish

AT THE BEGINNING OF THE WAR, THE BIGGEST DANGER TO MY immediate family was my mother. She almost blew up the house.

I'd better explain. One day, just after the bombing of Pearl Harbor by the Japanese, she announced that we had to stop eating canned food. I was horrified.

"Even tuna?" I asked her. I loved tuna sandwiches.

"Especially tuna!"

"Why?"

"A lot of canned fish and crabmeat came from Asia," she told me. "Especially from Japan."

"Japan? You think they might put bombs in cans of tuna?"

She reassured me about that, but said that there were rumors about the Japanese putting ground glass in the food that had been imported into the USA before Pearl Harbor. She went into the pantry and threw out every can that looked like it could have been anywhere near the Pacific Ocean. It was a big wrench for her. She hated to waste food. The result was that we stopped eating tuna and crabmeat for five years.

Also, to replace canned vegetables that she didn't trust either, we planted what people called a "Victory Garden" in our back yard. To help the war effort, everyone was being encouraged to grow their own food. So, we planted vegetables in every inch of our backyard. There were tomatoes, green beans, peas, green peppers and carrots.

Mother and I would go out to pick the food, and when we got to the carrots, we pulled them out of the ground and mother said we should eat them right then and there, dirt and all. She said that this was healthy, and would protect me from all sorts of diseases in the future. She told me, "You have to eat a pound of dirt before you die." Thanks to her, I'm pretty sure I ate my pound of dirt before I was ten.

We didn't eat all of our vegetables fresh, though. And this is where Mother's explosion enters the story.

One year, she made us pick all the tomatoes while they were still green. My father begged her to leave some to ripen, but she wouldn't listen, and I had to help her strip every tomato plant clean. Mom said she "had plans."

She bought a huge earthenware crock, like something that archeologists excavate from the ruins of an ancient Roman villa. She stood it in the corner of the kitchen, and got me to throw in every green tomato we had picked, pounds of them, of all sizes. Then, in our biggest saucepans, she boiled up bottle after bottle of vinegar with sugar and salt, and when the sweet-smelling mixture had cooled down, I helped to pour it all over the tomatoes. She covered the top with a tight muslin lid that she weighed down with a heavy pan. Then she stood back and proudly told me,

"Now we'll have pickled tomatoes all winter long."

Sadly, she was very wrong.

The crock stood there in the kitchen like a statue. Occasionally I would put my ear to the earthenware side, and was sure I could hear bubbling. But we weren't allowed to touch the crock or open the lid to see how the tomatoes were getting on.

A few weeks later, in the middle of the night, we and our neighbors were woken up by a massive bang. We thought it was a bomb. The firemen turned up, sirens blaring. The fire station was just down the street, and they'd heard the bang.

But when my father crept downstairs to investigate, he just found the whole kitchen splattered with shards of clay and lumps of over-fermented tomato. It turned out that the tomatoes had exploded.

Mother almost did the same thing with the wine she made from our Concord grape arbor. It went sour and turned into stinking raw alcohol. The problem was that Mother used to follow recipes in an old Jewish cookbook, but it didn't tell her when to stop things from pickling and fermenting.

It was lucky that Dad didn't get caught in Mom's explosion. Quite often, he was down in the kitchen during the night. He was an air raid warden, and his job was to go out on the street and make sure everybody had put down the shades in their house, so there was a complete blackout. Even in Boston, thousands of miles from Japan and Nazi Germany, we thought we might get bombed.

* * *

FOR US AS A FAMILY, apart from mother's attempts to demolish the house, the war was OK.

However, even though I was just a kid, I started to realize that outside of my immediate family, the war wasn't going so well for the Jews.

I used to go to the movies once or twice a month with my parents. They would take me to watch cartoons like *Dumbo* and *Bambi*, and kids' stories like *National Velvet* with little Elizabeth Taylor taming a wild horse (just as she would tame those wild husbands later).

Of course, every time, I would come out of the cinema saying I wanted a baby elephant, a deer or a black horse as a pet. And Dad said, sure, I could have a baby elephant, as long as I found one that could fly.

Once or twice I saw a war film. Not a battle picture, but one of those where the American serviceman is a good guy and comes home to his childhood sweetheart after saving the world.

But all of these movie programs started off with newsreels. And as the war went on, the tanks and airplanes started to get replaced by even scarier images. Thin, terrified faces of living skeletons. Kids with huge bewildered eyes and shaven heads. Barbed-wire fences, even piles of bodies. Sometimes Mom used to cover my eyes. And when I asked what these pictures meant, who the terrified people were, my parents looked deeply anxious and seemed to find it hard to explain.

Once, coming home from the movies in the car, I heard them talking about the newsreel we'd seen. They were discussing a woman who had been in charge of a place they called Buchenwald. (I only found out that name later, of course. At the time, it just sounded kind of Yiddish.) Mom said that this woman, called Ilse Koch, had made lampshades out of prisoners' skins after they were killed. Jewish prisoners, who had been locked up and starved just because they were Jewish.

Because she was deaf, Mom used to speak very loudly, so I could hear her clearly in the back seat of the car, over the engine noise. You can imagine the effect on a little girl of hearing these stories. To know that there were people like me getting massacred, just because, like me, they were Jewish. Imagine a little Boston girl going from thinking the biggest problem in the world was exploding tomatoes or Bambi's fictional Mom getting shot, to hearing that there were real people out there who really wanted to turn her into a lampshade.

My mother's parents knew what was going on in Nazi-occupied Europe, and were constantly worried about our relatives over in Riga, Latvia. Riga was occupied first by the Soviets, then by the Nazis.

My maternal grandfather was especially worried. He had come over on a boat from Latvia in the 1890s, when they tried to put all the young Jewish boys in the Russian army.

He arrived in New York, and first of all he went around with a sewing machine on his back, trying to make a living. He looked in a restaurant window and saw that the waiters were just ordinary guys who were carrying towels, so he went in and convinced the owner of the restaurant that he had experience as a waiter, and got the job. Then a friend of his was moving to Boston and needed a maître d', so he moved to Boston, eventually got into real estate, became very well off and got a house in Brookline. This is a very chic little town in Massachusetts, which at the time was home to a well-known American family, the Kennedys.

Even before the war, my grandfather was worried about the people he had left behind in Latvia. In 1937, with the Nazis on the rise and already stopping Jews doing business in Germany, my grandfather brought over a nephew from Riga. This nephew—my uncle—would visit me and my parents in Newton, and carry me around on his shoulders. In his cute accent he used to tell me that someday soon I would meet his little daughter who was my age, but still back in Latvia. She and his wife were coming over soon, he said.

Then war broke out, and nobody was allowed to leave Latvia. It wasn't till 1945 that he found out what happened to his family.

My uncle spoke five languages, so after the war, he joined UNRRA (the United Nations Relief and Rehabilitation Administration) to help take care of displaced persons. He went to Riga, and found out that his wife and daughter had initially been hidden from the Nazis at the beginning of the Occupation. However, finally the Nazis found them, and along with all the rest of the Jewish population of Riga, they were shot in the forest three miles away.

So, in 1945, as far as we knew, none of our European family had made it through the war. We were shocked, stunned, horrified. Who wouldn't be, to learn that their whole family had been massacred?

There was a twist to this story in the 1960s, but I'll talk about that later.

I will also explain in a later chapter why, as an adult, I have spent so much time going to Nazi concentration camps whenever I'm in Europe. I've been to Auschwitz, Dachau, Belsen, Buchenwald, and others. My friends ask me, why do I inflict all this horror upon myself? Well, I guess it's just that little girl still looking for the answer to the question: Why, why, why?

Chapter 3

Battling with Music

MY OWN CONTRIBUTION TO THE WAR EFFORT WAS MUSIC.

I had begun my career as a performer when I was five years old. My mother was suffering from pneumonia and was in bed upstairs, and I entertained myself by banging on the grand piano downstairs. Just like Beethoven, she couldn't hear too well, but she could feel the piano's vibrations, and she could tell I was making any old noise.

She called me into her room and asked me what I was doing.

"Playing the piano, Mom."

"No, you're not, you're demolishing it. Stop!"

She was too weak to get really mad, so for once I resisted.

"But I want to learn the piano, Mom. Then I'll be able to play songs for you."

"You'll only make me wish I was even more deaf."

"No, I won't, I promise, I'll learn to play really well."

"You'd better make it fast."

Anyway, that same day, she got my father to phone a piano teacher, Mrs. Wolfson, and ask her to come to the house once a week.

I remember my first lesson to this day.

Mrs. Wolfson was a kind lady with a soft voice and long fingers. She brought along a small briefcase, and pulled out a blue book that she gave to me, and told me to open it on to the stand above the piano keyboard. Then she sat me on the piano stool, with a cushion to lift me to the correct height, and explained that I was going to learn to play piano from this wonderful blue book—the Thompson Beginners' book.

"Will I play songs for my Mom?" I asked her.

"Not quite yet," she said, and showed me the first exercise.

So, for the next hour, I played C C C C C with my thumbs. First one thumb, then the other, then both thumbs at the same time. C C C C C. My poor mother upstairs must have been wishing she'd stopped me playing forever.

The second lesson was much more exciting for everybody concerned. I had to play C D E (right hand) and C B A (left hand). Again, first one hand, then the other, then—very difficult this time, and I kept getting it wrong—both hands together. Again, Mom must have thought that things would never get more tuneful.

But just as I promised her, I stuck at it. I went through that whole book in a year, and I was barely five years old.

It sounds impressive, but I had no choice in the matter, because as soon as my mother was cured of pneumonia, she started to make sure she was getting her money's worth with the lessons. If I didn't practice enough, she would hit me on the fingers with a ruler. Not too hard, just enough to remind me that it was better to suffer the pain of hard practice than the sting of a ruler on the back of my hand.

But I loved playing the piano, so she didn't need the ruler too often. As well as doing exercises, I would bang away at "Chopsticks", and then make up different versions of it for myself, changing the notes, playing the melody backwards or in harmony. I knew, though, that Mom and even kind Mrs. Wolfson wouldn't approve of me fooling around like this, forgetting my lessons and going off on exploratory tangents across the keyboard. And even I thought that it was a sin to change "real" music into something I'd invented myself, so I never played my versions to anyone except my dog, Bonnie. She used to sit there, blankly listening, obviously wondering when I would stop hammering on the big wooden box and take her out into the garden to play ball. But if only Bonnie had been more encouraging, and told me to go on improvising, I could have been a jazz player or maybe even a composer. What do dogs know about music? I've always wondered about that His Master's Voice logo.

As the war went on, I began to branch out musically.

Thanks to the newsreels, I'd started to hear patriotic tunes, and to understand that our troops always did better when there was a rousing band in the background, so I told Mom I wanted to learn a new instrument: the bass drum.

"The bass drum? But it's bigger than you are," she said.

"But I can learn it really quickly and be in the school marching band," I argued.

"You want to march with it? You can't even carry it! You'll have to roll along on top of it!"

But I persisted, so she let me try my hand on one of the school's bass drums. I was right—it was easy to learn. You just went bang in time to the music. My dog Bonnie could have done it. But Mom was right, too. I couldn't lift the drum.

So, I compromised and switched to the snare. That was a bit more challenging—you had to learn paradiddles and such-like—and much less heavy, but it was only a bit less boring, so I decided to try something less simple. I went over to see our neighbors, the Murphys, and asked to borrow their son Junie's trumpet. He was away in the Navy. It must have been a tough decision for them to lend out their son's instrument, but they kindly did so, and soon I was fighting on yet another musical front. And mother let me play whatever instrument I wanted as long as I kept taking classical piano lessons.

She kept telling me I was scaring away the Japanese bombers with my attempts to get a note out of the trumpet, so I should keep on playing. It was lucky for her she could hardly hear me making noises with that poor instrument that would have made Louis Armstrong faint.

Chapter 4

Stage Fright,
the Best Cure for Shyness

WHEN SHE WASN'T ALLOWING ME TO FILL THE HOUSE WITH TUNELESS noises, my mother's bad hearing was a constant embarrassment to me.

One time, she showed Mr. Murphy, who looked after our garden for us, the ants that were swarming over some of her favorite flowering plants.

He explained what the problem was, and told her he would come back later and deal with it. But my mother was impatient, and instead of waiting for him, she cut off all the buds from the plants.

When he came back, he told her, "No, I said we'd get rid of the *bugs*, not the *buds*."

Sometimes it wasn't so funny. The other children in my class would make fun of her and ostracize me. It wasn't until NASA started sending men into space, and made micro-instruments to transmit sound, that she had an operation to treat her deafness. It was a miracle for all of us in the family. After the first operation, she was upstairs in bed, and she screamed down saying that there was an awful noise in her bedroom. We ran up and found out that it was the ticking of the clock that she had never heard before.

Probably because my mother didn't socialize too much, I was a very shy child outside the home. I quickly realized that I found it difficult to talk to people I didn't know, but that there was no real reason why. I had perfect hearing, so why couldn't I put it to good use, and get into conversations? Again, just as I'd done with the piano, I put together a plan to improve myself.

First, I tried acting. In the third grade I auditioned for the starring role in our class play, *Peter Pan*.

I read the book, studied the illustrations, and made sure I could copy all the poses. I jumped off my bed and pretended to fly like a fairy. I even taught myself to play a couple of tunes on the recorder (I couldn't find any pan pipes).

At the audition, in front of two of my teachers, they got me to read some lines. Something about how I enjoyed living in some gardens with the fairies, because my parents didn't want me. I thought it all sounded a bit stupid (who wants to live in a garden when you can live in a house with a piano?) but I gave it my best shot.

The result was that I was offered the part of an old man, with just one line.

I went home crying to my mother.

"They didn't even ask me to walk around or pretend to fly!"

Mom listened to me, wiped my eyes, and told me not to worry.

"They gave you your first part, that's what's important," she said. "Show them you can do it really well, and next time you'll get a better part. Now what's the line?"

"It's a stupid line," I said.

"But what is it?"

"I'll save you, Wendy, but only if you pretend to be my mother."

"What?"

I wasn't sure if she hadn't heard me, or just didn't believe me, so I told her again, louder.

"I'll save you, Wendy, but only if you pretend to be my mother."

Neither of us knew why anyone would say something like that, but we practiced it, adding new variants until I'd turned my one line into a whole comic scene.

"I'll save you, Wendy!" Pause for dramatic effect. "But only..." Suspense, mischievous wink to the audience. "If you pretend to be..." Even more suspense, how could the audience bear it? "My mother!" Triumphant grin at my own wittiness.

I also rehearsed several different ways of hobbling round the stage like an old man, so I could attract attention to myself even when I wasn't delivering my unforgettable line. And on the day of the performance, my line was a massive hit. Even though Wendy refused my absurd offer to be her son, and made me look an idiot for suggesting it, I was sure the school would put together an offshoot of the show starring my character, who turned out to be called Mr. Smee. I could imagine the theme song: "Look at me, I'm Mr. Smee...." But nothing came of it. That's show business.

* * *

AS WELL AS HER EXCELLENT advice about rehearsing my one
line until it was perfect, my mother had some less helpful
things to say about my Peter Pan adventure.

"I know why they made you an old man," she told me.
"You're not feminine enough. You're not even feminine
enough to play Peter Pan!"

I knew what she meant. I was a real tomboy. I used to get
into fights with boys on the long walk to school. I used to go
out bicycling with the boys from the next street over. I got
myself a baseball mitt so I could join in their games, I even
played football with them. One thing I never did was play
with all the dolls that my family gave me, which I stuffed
away in cupboards and drawers.

"Why don't you play girls' games with girls?" Mom asked
me. "Then you'd be much more popular at school. They say
'boys will be boys', but they also think 'girls must be girls'."

But even then, that wasn't what I wanted from life. I
wanted to be me. Just a better version of me. A better piano
player, a more confident talker, a less painful trumpetist. I
wanted to show other people the best of me, and the perfect
place for that was on stage.

I thought that the best way to make myself popular
would be to play popular songs. I asked Mom if I could
learn some pop music on the piano, instead of the classical
stuff I was studying. Her initial reaction was not exactly
promising.

"Give up classical piano, after all the money I've spent on lessons? Never!"

"But some of the tunes in the musicals are just as difficult as classical pieces," I argued.

"Go and ask anyone in your class to hum Rachmaninov's Second Piano Concerto," she said. She had a point.

"But if I can play popular songs, I'll be more popular," I said.

This was an argument she could understand. She felt the pain of being left out because of her hearing, and she wanted to spare me from that.

"OK, here's the deal," she said. "You can learn popular songs with another teacher, as long as you carry on studying classical."

Of course, I accepted straight away. Twice as much piano? It was a double helping of heaven.

I was so excited that I learned my first pop songs really fast. There was "There's No Business Like Show Business" and "Doin' What Comes Naturally" from *Annie Get Your Gun*, the big hit musical of 1946. Knowing how to play these songs made a kid look very trendy back in the 1940s. Playing them in front of an audience also made you less shy, even if you were nervous inside. Only trouble was, playing the latest pop songs didn't necessarily make you more *popular*.

When I played them at school, people applauded, but when I got down from the piano, they didn't all say, "Hey, come and sit with us." The meaner kids even said I was showing off, or that I hadn't got the tune right. I told myself that they were just jealous, but it wasn't much of a consolation. And it didn't make me more friends. Some of the girlier girls even thought that hammering away at the piano was a bit too "masculine." There are some battles you can't win.

EVEN GETTING ON TV DIDN'T help. My first big showbiz opportunity came thanks to my uncle Larry Berk's music school, where I was having my pop music lessons.

Back then it was called the Schillinger House Music School, and it taught jazz and popular music. Television was in its infancy in the late 1940s, but the school hosted a live TV show on Sunday mornings. It was a kind of talent show called *Community Auditions*, sponsored by a local company, Community Opticians.

Maybe because I was the school owner's niece, I got a spot on the show. Well, *definitely* because I was the school owner's niece. What was the point of having a TV show if you didn't get your relatives on it?

The question was, what should I do? Play piano? No, because they had loads of piano players already, some of them really good at jazz. And remember, my dog Bonnie had killed off my jazz career years earlier. Play the trumpet? No, the TV show valued its microphones, and its viewers, too highly. Do Peter Pan? No, I only knew one line, and I couldn't make that last for a whole three-minute slot.

So, I had a think, and came up with an idea. The mime artist Marcel Marceau was very famous at the time, and I'd seen him in a movie newsreel. And with his white pasty face covered in make-up, he kind of looked like me at age 14. I'd seen him do his thing where he pretended he was stuck behind a big pane of glass. Now, I never really understood why he didn't just look for the door handle. All French windows have handles, right? And he was French, so he really should have known his way around French windows. But I liked the idea of pantomime. I'd been miming around when I played old Mr. Smee in Peter Pan. So, I thought maybe I could invent a scene that was more realistic than Marcel Marceau, and more me than the old man Mr. Smee. I could even make Mom happy and do something feminine.

Perhaps it was a sign of things to come later in my life, but I decided to do a striptease. I still have no clue where that idea came from. I probably just thought it was funny—I would be fully clothed but pretending to be naked. Ha ha ha. I was 14 at the time, remember, so I didn't know that this kind of thing went on for real in clubs. Of course, I wasn't really going to take one single item of clothing off in public—I was much too shy. Even so, I didn't tell Mom or my uncle what I was planning to do. I just said, "I'll do a pantomime," and they said "Great!" They probably imagined me getting stuck behind a pane of glass.

So that Sunday morning, I went along to the studio, which was just a big room with a barrage of huge lights pointed at a stage, as if they were going to interrogate us. There were two cameras, like giant-headed robots on tripods, that were going to conduct the interrogation. And at the back of the room, about ten rows of uncomfortable wooden seats where the audience was going to sit—the audience being all the performers waiting to go on, and their families. Mom, Dad and my brother were sitting in the front row.

Make-up was a girl with a powder puff, and she rubbed it on my face, then I went to sit nervously with my family.

The show began—it was live, of course, nothing was recorded in those days—and a presenter came on and told everyone how he got his glasses from Community Opticians, then introduced the first act. It was a kid playing "There's No Business Like Show Business" on the piano, and I thought, I could have done that. Then a girl came on, tap dancing to a jazzy number, and I was very impressed until she slipped and fell over, and I thought, I would have done that. Then they told me to get ready because I was on next, and after the presenter had told everyone that his wife looked beautiful in her glasses, and he knew because he could see her close up thanks to *his* glasses, I was on TV.

My music started. When I'd said I was going to do pantomime, my uncle said, "OK, we'll give you some French music," so I started stripping to the sound of an accordion. How was I to know that that would make lots of adults think of Paris and sex?

I'd rehearsed some comedy material, like getting stuck pulling my blouse over my head, and falling over when I took off my shoes. And the audience laughed, but kind of nervously. Here was a tiny 14-year-old doing a Parisian strip-club act.

I looked coy when I got down to my underwear, and I thought it was funny to wriggle out of my panties, but I guess it was embarrassing to the audience. Especially to my poor mother. There she was, hoping her daughter was going to become more popular by going on TV, and now the girl was disgracing the whole family.

I didn't understand that while I was stripping, of course. To me, taking off my imaginary panties live on TV was just funny.

And then, the finale to my act. I got in the shower, turned on the water, and it was too cold. Oh! That was freezing! The audience laughed, probably out of relief. To me, it sounded like sweet confirmation that pantomime was my new direction. My first mime—taking a shower—had been a smash hit.

I came off, as the presenter told the cameras that they could get cleaning fluid from Community Opticians if their glasses had steamed up, and ran to my family. Instead of the congratulations I expected, Dad was shaking his head, my brother was grinning as if he'd just seen me smash a vase, and Mom was about to explode.

Dad said to me, "Why didn't you speak?" He'd obviously never seen Marcel Marceau.

Mom was less curious.

"Out!" she said, much too loud, and one of the production guys tried to quiet her down. She grabbed my wrist and whisked me away, clomping across the floor in her big shoes, making all the TV people tear their hair out as the presenter tried to talk over the noise.

"What's wrong, Ma?" I asked as soon as we were out in the corridor. I didn't get it at all. I'd been a hit, hadn't I? They'd laughed.

"Taking your clothes off in public!" She pulled me towards the stairs.

"I didn't take my clothes off. It was pantomime!"

"A French striptease!"

I didn't even know what that was.

"I was just taking a shower, Ma!"

"On TV!"

I was so naïve, it wasn't until fifteen years later, when I actually went to a Parisian strip club, that I understood why Mom was mad. The strippers there didn't end up in the shower, but they sure wriggled when it came down to the underwear.

I doubt if I helped to sell more glasses, but I do know that my uncle's school certainly flourished after my first TV appearance. The Schillinger House School subsequently changed its name, to become the Berklee School of Music, after my uncle and his son, and it is now one of the most popular music schools in the world. I just hope that in some small way my striptease act paved the way for the school's success.

MY SHOWBIZ CAREER DEVELOPED FURTHER in junior high—though not that much further. I got the lead role in a mystery play, but only because they needed the character to be small, so she could be carried when she was sick. But at least it was a female lead, and Mom was happy because I didn't pretend to take my clothes off.

She was less happy with my next performance, though most of my fellow students were highly delighted.

The school held a declamatory contest, and my drama coach suggested I should learn a poem about being a strong and forceful person.

"It will help you affirm your personality," he said. "I know the perfect text for you."

So I let him choose the poem—big mistake. It was "Another Chance" by an American poet called Henry van Dyke. (Little did I know that the effect on my audience was going to be more in the style of Dick van Dyke).

It was really long, but the drama coach said I should learn only the first section, a "mere" sixteen lines. It was all about being spared death and given a chance to prove yourself. Comic it was not.

"My dreams were always beautiful, my thoughts were high and fine; No life was ever lived on earth to match those dreams of mine."

It was all inspiring, tear-jerking stuff like that. I memorized my lines, and auditioned for a couple of the schoolteachers, who said I was ready to perform at the contest.

The big day came, and the whole school was there in a huge auditorium, and my parents came along to see me recite my character-building poem. I was excited, confident, determined to do a good job.

When my turn came, I went out on stage and recited, word perfect. I was feeling great as I finished with a flourish on my big last line:

"Another chance is all I need, to prove myself a man."

At which point, every student in the auditorium burst out laughing.

I almost started crying, but as soon as I said it, I realized they were right. This little girl, this tomboy, announcing that she wanted to become a *man*? Back then, no one spoke about changing gender, so it was just plain hilarious.

I turned as red as one of Mom's tomatoes and rushed off stage, where all the other performers were looking horrified.

They were scared I'd broken the spell for them. Now anyone who went out on that stage could be laughed at!

Mom wasn't laughing when she picked me up outside the stage door.

"What are you trying to do to me?" she wailed. "I'm doing my best to turn you into a young woman, and you're turning yourself into a man!"

"But it was my drama teacher who chose the poem," I defended myself.

"Your ex-drama teacher, you mean," she said. And that was the end of him.

LUCKILY, MOM WASN'T THERE TO see my next stage role. It was while I was at Camp Tawamana, in New Hampshire, with the girl scouts. And it was a male lead. Surprise, surprise.

This was in 1948, and the scout leaders decided to put on a singing, dancing version *Hansel and Gretel*. For some reason, they gave me the part of Hansel, and I was thrilled. We rehearsed for days on end, and I got to sing, dance, clown around, in front of an audience of cheering, clapping friends who obviously loved me. I was wearing trousers, and being as masculine as I could, but no one cared. Those girl scout camps were early experiments in gender fluidity.

Every summer, we had what they called Heart Sister Day. We picked out a piece of paper that had one of the other girl's names on it, kept it a secret, and were supposed to leave gifts and messages and cards and candy all day on her bunk bed when she wasn't around.

My first Heart Sister was Mabel. I was delighted, because she was one of the cutest girls at camp. She was tall, with a mature figure, and wavy chestnut hair. But unlike some of the cute girls at my school, she wasn't arrogant or stand-offish. So it felt really natural to leave some of the candy I'd brought from home under her pillow, and to draw her a giant red heart. It was just teenage girls being nice to each other, right?

At the same time, of course, I was being complimented by a mystery girl. I found a juicy apple on my bed (very Adam and Eve), and a poem that went something like "Diana I'm your fana"—it was funny and made me blush all over with pleasure.

At supper, it was a big surprise for everyone when we found out who our Heart Sister was. Mabel gave me a friendly kiss on the cheek, and I went and hugged the girl who'd sent me the poem. Her name was Rachel, and I didn't know her well before that, but for the rest of that summer we were inseparable friends.

I think those camps were a really formative part of my youth. It was great training for me later on in life, when I had genuine girlfriends. I would treat them to gifts and messages just like I'd done for my Heart Sisters. As I look back at the two girl scout camps that I went to, I am beginning to think that most of the counselors were gay.

Who cares, though? The camp counselors never interfered with us, and they gave us every opportunity to camp it up on stage, as boys or girls. I felt much freer and happier there than I did at home and at school. There was no disapproval. I even did my shower striptease pantomime, and the camp counselors loved it.

* * *

BACK AT SCHOOL, I TRIED changing my musical direction to make myself more popular—this time, with boys. Every girl's goal at school was to get dates with boys, and I wanted to fit in. I'd already joined the school band and orchestra as a trumpet player, and now I became the solo trumpeter.

But it was like when I'd first played the piano. Success in the school band didn't get me dates. I really didn't understand why not. To become solo trumpeter, I'd beaten out a guy in my class who eventually went on to play in the Boston Symphony Orchestra. He was very talented, but apparently, I was even more so. Why didn't that make me good dating material?

I had a think about this and decided to blame the trumpet.

I told Mom I was going to stop trumpet lessons.

"Just when you're getting good?" she said. Then, straight away, "Good idea. You'll never get a date if you play trumpet. Name me one woman who plays trumpet."

For once I agreed with her, so I went to explain to my trumpet teacher.

"Sorry, but I'm going to stop taking lessons."

"Why? Just when you're getting really good!"

"I can't wear lipstick when I play trumpet. I need to wear lipstick if I'm going to get dates."

"So, what are you going to play?"

I hadn't thought that through yet. I said the first thing that came into my head: "Glockenspiel."

"Yes," Junie said, "such a sexy instrument."

He was right. From then on, I wore lipstick and played glockenspiel. But still the boys at Newton High didn't like me any better.

THE DATING SCENE FINALLY GOT a bit hotter for me in my senior year. Though by today's standards, it was pretty tepid. And compared to what I was going to get up to a few years later in Paris, it was ice cold.

The problem was that I was so incredibly innocent. In high school we took a sex course in our senior year. (Not a practical course, you understand—just theory.) A female teacher taught the girls, and a male taught the boys. There were diagrams of human bodies that didn't make you think of sex at all. They looked more like instructions on how to cut up meat. And the only concrete thing I remember from it is that one of the girls in the class asked what we were allowed to do before we got married. And all the teacher would say was "don't let the boys put their tongues in your mouths."

I STARTED TO GET A few dates with guys from Harvard and MIT. Even if they weren't very good-looking or interesting, my mother and my friends said this was the thing to do. A Boston girl couldn't do any better than marry a graduate from one of the top schools. It was only later that I realized that guys with lower IQs actually have something to offer a woman. All my parents wanted was to marry me off to a boy with a great career ahead of him. No one seemed to care about *my* career.

My favorite date of the time was David Gorfinkle. He was a student at Harvard. He used to take me out to the most popular venue at the time, the Totem Pole Ballroom in Norumbega Park, Boston. We called it "the Pole". This was a huge ballroom, with a big stage where a 20-piece jazz orchestra would be playing, and everyone was smartly dressed—the men in suits and ties with slicked-back hair, the girls in their best dresses. We would dance (a foxtrot, followed by a foxtrot and another foxtrot), and then go to sit in semi-darkness on deep, soft velvet couches with high sides to make them feel very private. It was very romantic and terribly innocent. There was no alcohol, no petting, not even any jitterbugging. We drank soft drinks and danced cheek-to-cheek, and talked.

I invited David Gorfinkle to my senior prom, which was held there. He came along in his tux, his hair oiled and neatly parted, his bow tie slightly crooked. He was very cute, the perfect date. We had a wonderful evening, and he gave me a fantastic gift. No, not a diamond brooch or some silk lingerie. It was a Webster's New Collegiate Dictionary, 1949 edition. I loved it. It was my first dictionary, and I still use it today.

Back then, maybe I should have used it more, to look up "sex", or even "making out", to see what it was all about. Maybe David was disappointed with our tepid dates, I don't know. My parents were old friends of his parents, and they hoped that sparks would fly. There were no sparks, but I did get a dictionary. Life has its compensations.

Chapter 5

The Secrets of College Life

DURING MY JUNIOR YEAR IN HIGH SCHOOL, I STARTED TO LOOK into where I would go to college. In 1951 I went on a bicycle trip with the American Youth Hostel Association across America and Canada. I visited Stanford University in California and then Reed College up in Oregon. I liked Reed and learned that they had an excellent Drama Department.

I came home and told my parents all about it.

"Reed?" Dad said. "Isn't that a liberal college?"

"Liberal? Liberal!?" When Mom really wanted to hear something, she heard. "You used to do a striptease without anyone asking you. If you study drama at a liberal college, they'll get you stripping off for real every day! Where is Reed, anyway?"

"Portland, Oregon," I told her.

"Portland? Oregon?" She made it sound as if it was on another planet. Which, culturally, it was.

By now they were both shaking their heads. A liberal college, far away in Oregon, studying drama? It was as if I'd ticked the three wrong boxes on a job application form. Alcoholic, drug addict, criminal record? Tick, tick, tick.

"Why don't you apply to Dartmouth?" Dad said. "New Hampshire would be perfect for winter sports."

"They don't accept women," I said.

This was the case for plenty of good American colleges at the time.

"Just find yourself a nice college that accepts Jews and women, and isn't too far from Boston," Mom said. "And not too expensive."

Simple.

In the end, we found one—Middlebury, a small New England co-ed college, which had its own ski area. We heard it was a bit preppy and WASPy, so I didn't think I had much chance of getting in, but lo and behold, I was accepted. I was thrilled!

However, as soon as I got there, I found out that out of 2,000 students, I was the only Jewish girl in the whole college, and there were only a few Jewish boys. WASPy was an understatement. The college had even put on an all-gentile version of *Fiddler on the Roof*. One of the students told me she didn't know any Jews, but she'd "seen some at the beach."

I phoned home and told my father how strange it felt.

"I don't understand how I even got accepted at Middlebury," I said.

"You can thank me for that," he said. "I met a trustee of the college at a cigar smokers' club. He pulled a few strings."

"Oh, thanks, Dad. You got me into a college where the only Jews they know are ones they saw at the beach. What are we, jellyfish?"

"The first of a wave, I'm sure. You're opening up the way for everyone."

He made it sound very idealistic, but when he came and visited me at Middlebury, all he said was, "I've never seen so many blonde girls all in one place." Very idealistic.

NEEDLESS TO SAY, IN THAT WASPy, segregated social context, I didn't date much. I stayed in the dorm every Saturday night while my friends went to frat parties to which I wasn't invited. And I wasn't allowed to join a sorority—they didn't let Jews in. I wasn't even invited to meet the sorority members at a party. I was heartbroken.

To make myself more popular, I tried to be a little daring. At the end of my junior year, I got invited to perform in the Variety show in front of the whole school.

I asked myself, what act should I do? Some music, maybe? But the danger was, I wouldn't be cool enough. A lot of the students were a lot more hip to jazz than I was. A monologue, maybe? It would have to be funny, and I didn't know any comedy routines. Then I remembered: there was one routine I'd done before, and that might go down well in this sophisticated environment.

I went on stage and, while giving thanks that Mom wasn't in the audience, I did my pantomime of undressing and taking a shower. I played up the comedy and the wriggling, and to make it hip, I chose some accompaniment from a new movie, *Singin' in the Rain*. It worked fine. At first, the audience were wondering why I would take my clothes off during an innocent Gene Kelly movie, and at the end, I was showering in the musical rain. A great punchline, and the students laughed. I was relieved. At last, people appreciated my sense of humor. Or so I thought.

The following year, I wasn't invited to be on the show again. And when I went along to watch the dress rehearsal one day, one of the newer students told me that the year before, there had been a scandalous pantomime of some girl taking her clothes off—so the college had made sure that this year's show was going to be much "cleaner".

I just didn't fit in.

OH WELL, AT LEAST I got in a lot of skiing and mountain climbing (of course I didn't mention to Mom that I was specializing in what she would have called "masculine" pursuits).

And in my second year, I moved to live in the dorm they called the French Chateau, where we had to speak French, and French majors came to have dinner with us so they could practice.

The dinner guests were both male and female, and one evening, a guy was watching me all through the meal.

Afterwards, he came up to me and whispered, "Are you Jewish?"

"Why would you ask me that?" I said. I knew that people had got into lots of trouble for answering "yes" to that particular question.

"You didn't eat the ham."

"I don't like ham. I love rice, though. Does that make me a Hindu?"

He laughed.

"Come on, I'm Jewish, too. And I'm like you, almost scared to tell anyone. But I've had enough of hiding. They won't let us join their clubs, so let's start a Hillel."

"What's a Hillel?"

"It a Jewish organization that some colleges have. We can start one, and you can be president."

"Doesn't there have to be a vote?"

"There's only two of us, so if you vote for yourself, it's unanimous."

"Can you have a Hillel with only two people?"

"That's just the start. Did you know there are ten Jewish guys in the college?"

"Ten?" My father was right, it was turning into a wave.

"With you, that makes eleven."

"There's another Jewish girl, too."

"Twelve? Where will we find a room big enough to meet? We'll have to build a Hillel building!"

It was fun to find someone who could joke about such a sensitive subject with me. So, we two started the Hillel at Middlebury, and I was voted president, two votes to zero, and then we recruited new members. But not everyone was ready to come out as Jewish—at first it was just me, the other Jewish girl and six of the boys.

But if you're thinking we got together in our own fraternity-sorority to enjoy drinking, drugs, parties and sex, it was nothing like that. If anything, we became more religious. I realized that maybe this was why the other Jewish guys didn't want to join. They were having too much fun. We asked a Jewish professor from the University of Vermont to come down on Sundays and talk to us about history and culture. It was very educational, but not exactly exciting. I realized I needed other ways to express myself.

NEXT TIME I WENT HOME for the vacation, I talked about my lack of social and artistic life with Mom.

"Join the choir," she said.

"But I don't have a good voice."

"No, that's true. Even I can hear that."

"Thanks a lot, Mom."

But she was right. When I had performed pop songs at school, I was kind of speaking them. So Mom organized singing lessons for me when I went back to college.

One evening, a Mr. Peterson from Green Mountain Junior College came over to Middlebury, and we went into the music room. I sat at the piano and he told me to sing a song.

I immediately went into "Annie Get Your Gun," doing what came naturally, which was a low semi-speaking voice.

He stopped me after the first couple of lines.

"No, I really want to hear you *sing*."

He put a book of old songs on the piano and pointed to "Drink to Me Only with Thine Eyes." I looked at the music, played a few notes, and shook my head.

"I can't sing that high. Can we try it in a lower key?"

"Just try."

He sat down at the piano, played the introduction, and I launched into the song. And out came this voice that I had never heard before. It was high and strong, almost operatic. I was amazed!

Mr. Peterson was all smiles.

"You have a wonderful natural voice. You should audition for the choir as an alto."

I thought he was crazy, but we rehearsed different songs for a couple of weeks, and then I went to the choir master, a French guy called Monsieur Bergé, and asked to audition.

He said OK, so I sang him my operatic version of "Drink to Me Only with Thine Eyes", and he said, "Perfect, you're in." I was accepted! I was so astonished that I had an attack of nerves.

"I don't think I can do it," I told him.

"Why not?"

"Well, it's a Presbyterian choir that sings Christian services for the college on Sundays. "

"So?"

"So, I'm Jewish."

"Oh." He nodded as though he understood the problem, and I thought I was going to be thrown out of the choir already. But then after a few seconds, he added, "Me too, don't tell everyone. I told them I'm French, but my real name is Berger."

This was crazy. I wondered how many of us were hiding at Middlebury, concealing our identity so that we could seem to fit in.

"Come and join us, you'll be great," he told me.

Even so, I felt that I had to clear it with my mother. I went to a public call box so nobody would overhear, and called her up.

Shouting down the telephone so she would hear, I told her, "Mom, I got accepted in the choir."

"That's wonderful, Diana, well done."

"But there's a problem."

"You can't sing?"

"Thanks, Mom. No, the choirmaster says I have an excellent alto voice. But the choir sings almost nothing but Christian hymns."

"Oh." She had a quick think about this. "No problem: just hum when they talk about Jesus."

"Hum?"

"Yes, don't sing the Christian words. You can sing about God all you want, just don't mention Christ. Hum every time he crops up in a song."

I'm not sure this was how religion was meant to be, but I figured it was like my father tying the Christmas tree under the car. A small compromise, to fit in.

SO, FOR THE NEXT THREE years, every Sunday during teatime, I sang in the Middlebury chapel choir, standing in the front row, and going: "Onward mm-mm soldiers, marching as to war, with the mm of mm-mm, going on before ..."

It was only at a college reunion fifty years later that I found out that one of the other choir members, Sy Marchand, had noticed what I was doing, and secretly did exactly the same thing.

Incidentally, I also found out at that reunion that the only other female member of my Hillel at Middlebury, Nancy, who was my Maid of Honor at my wedding in 1958, was a lesbian.

So many secrets.

Chapter 6

Learning Much More in France

SINCE I HAD TAKEN ORAL FRENCH AT COLLEGE FOR TWO years (without learning anything about French kissing, I should add), I applied to spend the summer of 1955 in France with a group called The Experiment in International Living.

Sadly, they answered that the basic requirement was to have studied four years of French, so you could speak well enough with your host family. I really wasn't capable of chatting in any foreign language but I got my French professor to send a letter saying that I was very conversational in French, and in the end, I was accepted.

My destination was to be Belfort, in the east of France near Alsace and the Swiss border. Great, I thought, wine *and* chocolate.

Airplane travel was not so common in 1955, so we crossed the Atlantic by sea, on a Dutch ship out of Quebec. For five days we had lectures on French culture and what to expect when we got to France, and I even tasted champagne for the first time. I realized that the Old World was going to be a whole new world for me.

When we arrived in Paris, we went directly to our hotel on rue Monge, in the Latin Quarter, where five of us virginal girls were allotted to one room. I didn't realize it, but it was probably so we could defend each other against the men.

In one corner of the room was a normal washbasin, below a mirror, and beside it, lower down, stood a basin that looked a bit like a toilet. None of us had ever seen a bidet before.

"What is that thing?" we asked each other. There were various theories.

"It's in case there's someone else on the other toilet."

"It's a drinking fountain." Well, there was a kind of water jet that spouted upwards.

"No, it's for your feet."

So, WE ASKED OUR GUIDE, Michael. He looked a little embarrassed.

I had a guess: "Is it to wash our underwear?"

He gave a smile.

"Well, it is supposed to help keep your underwear clean."

He wouldn't say any more. I for one was none the wiser.

That first evening, we went to Les Halles, the area of old market halls in the center of the city. There were hundreds of food trucks being loaded and unloaded by men wearing blue overalls and yelling at each other. In a café there, we had onion soup and *escargots*.

Then we went to the Eiffel Tower, up to the second floor, and then walked down on to the quay beside the Seine. It was July, the moon was shimmering on the river, and we all danced and sang the Cole Porter song "I Love Paris."

I fell in love with Paris as I was dancing on the riverbank. It's the only love affair that has lasted all my life.

As well as the snails, the bidet and the Eiffel Tower, I was experiencing something else that was very new: predatory men. Back home in Boston, and even at college, the guys had been reserved and respectful. *Too* damn respectful. They'd behaved like trainee priests. Here in Paris, though, the men in the street smiled at you, winked at you, came on to you.

"Bonsoir, Mademoiselle, where are you going?" ... "You are so *jolie*, Mademoiselle, come and have a drink with me?" ... "Oh, Mademoiselle, my life will not be complete if you do not have dinner with me tonight."

It was flattering, but it was scary too. These guys weren't all movie stars. Some of them were old, ugly, creepy. And they wouldn't take "*non merci*" for an answer.

We asked Michael, what can we say to make them go away? (Well, the creepy ones, anyway.) He told us to say "fous le camp."

"What does that mean?" we asked.

"Go away, please."

We rehearsed.

"Fool con! Fool con, Monsieur. Fool con!"

What I didn't find out till much later was that it basically meant "go fuck yourself." Which was effective, but, as I also found out on my next trip to France a few years later, it was a really stupid thing to say. These Parisians didn't need to go fuck themselves. They were all fucking each other.

***

BUT BACK TO 1955. AFTER just three days of Paris, we took the train to Belfort, to meet our host families. I was with Monsieur and Madame Dreyfus and their son, 14-year-old Jean-Pierre. I slept on the top floor of the big house, and when I woke up the next morning, I was amazed to hear people outside talking in a language I didn't understand. Then I remembered I was in France.

I went down to breakfast, to find Monsieur and Madame Dreyfus and Jean-Pierre sitting at a big wooden table in the kitchen, clearly waiting for me.

I smiled at everyone and went to sit in the fourth seat.

Monsieur Dreyfus stopped smiling and started to rant at me. I wondered if I'd been snoring in the night, or maybe I should have used the bidet before breakfast. I finally understood that he was mad at me because I didn't say the usual pre-breakfast greeting. He got me to repeat.

"Bonjour," he said.

"Bon jaw," I attempted.

"Vous avez bien dormi?" (Did you sleep well?).

"Voo savvy band or me?"

"Oui, merci."

"Wee mercy."

He told me that in France, politeness is really important. Though he obviously didn't think he had to explain it to me very politely.

It turned out that Monsieur Dreyfus was a typically conservative provincial Frenchman. He was Jewish, but had married a Catholic woman and turned typically Catholic.

"Where are you going today?" He asked me, in French of course.

"Well, this morning, I...."

Before I'd finished my hesitant French phrase, he interrupted me.

"You must be back here for lunch at thirteen hours."

"Thirteen?" It was like the army. He meant one o'clock, of course.

"And what will you do in the afternoon?"

"Well, this afternoon, I...."

"You must be back here at nineteen hours."

I worked this out. Seven o'clock? But the night was still young. No, not young, at seven it hadn't even been born yet.

"Well, this evening...." I started to explain my plans to meet up with my friends.

"This evening you will be at home."

"But...."

"Your parents told me to be very strict. Every evening, you will be here at home. I don't know what you have been doing in America, but here in Belfort...." He raised a finger towards the ceiling, as if Belfort was another name for heaven.

I was like a prisoner. I wanted to tell him that I was 21 and a senior at college. No one was supposed to tell me to stay in at night. He had to let me go out! But I was too polite—and too bad at French—to do so.

* * *

LUNCH AND DINNER TIMES WERE just as strict as breakfast. I had to learn to put my hands on the table instead of on my lap, and the order of the meal was always the same—salad, then the main course, then cheese, maybe dessert. The only consolation was that there was always wine. Back home, I never drank anything alcoholic, because my parents didn't allow it, but Monsieur Dreyfus was very strict about making me drink wine with every meal. That was my kind of strictness. What an education I was having. I spent most of those evenings at home with a mildly drunk smile on my face.

Sometimes at dusk, I was allowed to go out walking with him and his friends, but he would get mad if I laughed or spoke too loudly. He said that in France you have to be quieter than in America. (I don't know where he got that idea. No one I've ever met in France tried to be quiet.)

During the day, my American group would have trips and meetings with all our French "brothers and sisters." Jean-Pierre came along, and we went cycling a couple of times, so we could go swimming in a lake nearby. While we dried off in the sun, I asked him to teach me more French, and he started me off on my long career of learning rude words. This was much more fun than his father's session at breakfast.

"Shit is merde."

"Med."

"No, merrrrde!" He repeated it with all the throat-clearing you need to do if you're going to pronounce the French "R" properly.

"Putain."

"Poo tan."

"No, pu-TA!" This was an exclamation that meant whore, but also "damn!" when you were annoyed at something.

"Fous le camp!"

"Fool con!" This one I knew.

"Très bien," Jean-Pierre said, "now you can be as insulting as a Frenchman. Just remember never to say any of those things in front of my papa."

THE SECOND MONTH OF THE trip was touring all of France by bicycle, about 60 miles a day, and camping out. The idea was to take our French "brothers and sisters" with us. But when we discussed the idea over breakfast one day, Monsieur and Madame Dreyfus didn't want to let Jean-Pierre go.

"My parents would prefer him to come with us," I said, which was a lie. They didn't want me going anywhere near a French boy after dark.

"He always comes on vacation with us, to his grandparents' house," Madame Dreyfus said.

Jean-Pierre shot me a pleading look. Apparently, a month with his parents and grandparents wasn't his idea of a fun time.

"My parents will be very happy if Jean-Pierre continues to teach me French."

Of course, I didn't tell them what kind of French he was teaching me. My vocabulary was getting pretty rich by now.

"Very well," Monsieur Dreyfus finally said.

To thank me, that afternoon Jean-Pierre taught me a key piece of French swearing.

"To insult an idiot, you can say 'con'," he told me. "This is a vulgar word. In fact, it is the women's—you know." He gestured down between his legs. He meant it was the French equivalent of the c-word, something I don't think I'd ever heard said in English before. "But if the idiot is a woman," he told me, "you must change the word. 'Con' becomes 'conne'."

"I don't get it," I said. "If it's a woman, you have to change the word for the woman's—you know?"

"Yes, 'con' is masculine."

"Wow, that's sexism for you."

"So, repeat after me: Monsieur vous êtes un con... Madame vous êtes une conne."

I repeated it for him, though I didn't think I'd get much chance to use that kind of phrase during my time camping with my fellow college students.

I was wrong. During that whole camping trip, Jean-Pierre turned into a real 'con'. As soon as he was away from his strict upbringing, he was wild, and made trouble for everyone. The first night, on the train to Avignon, he kept fooling around and wouldn't let any of us sleep. While we were camping, he never did any of the work to prepare the campsite. There wasn't exactly that much to do because we didn't have tents. We were just rolling out our sleeping bags in fields, but Jean-Pierre didn't even help us to make a fire or cook dinner. He was immature, even for a French teenage boy, and I regretted persuading his parents to let him come with us.

* * *

FORTUNATELY, WE HAD SOME REALLY good times, too.

In Avignon—guess what—we sang on the bridge. Then we cycled west across the South of France, sleeping and cooking over a fire in fields or wherever we could camp. We went to Pau, Ortez, and finally to Biarritz on the Atlantic coast—a trip of almost 400 miles. By the end of it, I could have won the Tour de France. As long as not too much of it was uphill.

During this long trip, I realized how different French and American kids were about physical things. When we were camping, the French kids got dressed and undressed in front of everybody. They didn't care. Up to certain limits, of course. They didn't run around naked. But we Americans would go off and hide to get changed. No wonder my striptease pantomime had shocked everyone. I, of course, did my best to adopt the French attitude—and I've never stopped.

I was also sad to see how lazy most of my Americans friends were. They kept to themselves, while I went off with the French kids to shop, and then helped out with the cooking. All the French kids, except Jean-Pierre, were great fun to be with. I loved the way we would all joke together and have fun, even when we were doing the chores. I felt fully accepted and happy. My French friends didn't ask where my grandparents came from, or what religion I was. I had never had this experience in America, of fitting in with the crowd. I fell in love with France and the French that summer, and it's a feeling I've never lost.

After Biarritz, we Americans headed back to Paris, and as soon as I got there, I decided to drop the group, and wander around by myself. I'd got a taste of being French, and wanted to enjoy it some more.

This time, I didn't tell the Parisian guys to "fous le camp", and I got picked up. But I must have disappointed them with my naivety. Even when I was in a café near the Arc de Triomphe, necking a bit, I wouldn't let the guy kiss me. I remembered my lesson from school —I'd been warned about French kissing. You never knew what kind of disease you could pick up from some random guy's tongue. And I was especially wary of these Parisian tongues, which seemed to do a lot of kissing.

One guy I met took me to a spot near Pigalle where there were prostitutes standing in the street, soliciting passers-by. "Tu montes, chéri?" This was what they said to the men—are you coming upstairs?

I'd never seen anything like it. These women, some of them with skirts split up to the thigh, with low-cut tops showing almost everything they'd got to offer, were shaking their hips at the men and offering themselves. Any guy would do. I was shocked by the openness of it all.

The Parisian guy grinned and asked what I thought. He was probably hoping I'd get turned on by it all, and change from a naïve Bostonian who didn't want to kiss him into an insatiable vamp.

"It's immoral," I told him. "The men are just walking by, and might get tempted, and catch a disease." Well, I said as much of this as my knowledge of French would let me.

"They're not just walking past," he said. "They've come here to look, and maybe choose a girl." He called them "filles," though some of them were as old as my grandmother.

"Why don't they just get married?" I asked. I was speaking for myself, of course. I'd been told that sex didn't happen until after the vows.

He laughed.

"Here in France, if you want sex, you can get it easily. It's not so expensive. You get what you pay for."

I was even more shocked. "Have you been with a prostitute?"

He laughed again, and didn't answer.

"In America, there are a lot more sex crimes because prostitution is against the law," he said.

I didn't know how to answer that. Of course, I didn't know back then that there were just as many rapes in France as anywhere else, but he probably didn't care what I thought. He just wanted some of that Pigalle sexiness to rub off on me. Well, he was out of luck. For the time being, anyway.

I said a quick "au revoir" and left him to walk the pavement, check out the "filles" on offer and probably find one in his price range.

Another thing that shocked me, but less than the prostitution, was something I noticed in Saint Germain des Prés, where the philosophers used to hang out in the 1940s and 1950s, talking about how morally superior they were to everyone else.

I used to sit on the café terraces with a cheap coffee and watch the passers-by, as everyone else was doing. It was surprising that there was anyone left over to do the passing-by.

Maybe they took it in turns. "You sit on the terrace, I'll walk by. Now it's your turn to walk while I sit and watch."

And several times I saw girls dressed like boys. Not just in pants and a shirt, but really dressed up like a man, in a men's suit, for example, with a tie. I had never seen this in America. Just like what I'd seen in Pigalle, I was shocked. But this time, the shock was less disapproving. I was surprised and intrigued and couldn't stop thinking about it. I thought the girls in men's clothing looked very attractive. I didn't know what to do about this feeling, but I filed it away for future use.

Chapter 7

Back to America with a Bump

BACK IN COLLEGE, I SPENT A WEEK IN THE INFIRMARY, AND THEN stayed depressed for all my senior year. I missed my French friends and my French freedom. They had made me realize that life in Middlebury was deeply uninteresting. I'd found out that I could be who I wanted to be in France, whereas in a preppy New England college, I was a *poisson* out of water. Even then, I knew I had to get back across the Atlantic to those free-running, energizing waters of France.

So, I graduated from Middlebury with my BA in Drama and French, but I didn't know how to use it. I lacked all the knowledge and sophistication to become a French drama queen.

I decided I needed to keep studying. Back in Boston, I told my parents, "I thought I'd apply to law school and become a lawyer like Daddy."

They both said, "No. No. No!" At least that was clear.

"Why not?"

"You'll be too smart and no guy would marry you," Dad said. Welcome to the 1950s.

"The idea of going to college wasn't to get a BA," Mom explained. "It was to get an MRS."

"An MRS?"

"Yes, a missus, meaning a diploma that will make a girl look marriageable to an educated man."

Well, they were paying for my education—or lack of it—so I had to give in. The only choices they offered me were teaching, nursing or secretarial work. So, I went to secretarial school for a year where all I learned was fake shorthand. I couldn't figure out the squiggles. But I was a quick notetaker, and typed fast, so I got through. And in the spring of 1957, that diploma got me a job as the worst secretary ever.

I got an interview to be the secretary to the President of the Jewish Vocation Service, Dr. Fineburg.

I sat in his office, and he looked me over, and seemed to approve. I got the impression I wasn't just being inspected for signs of weakness or illness.

"Can you do shorthand?" he eventually asked me.

"I just finished a year's course at secretarial college," I said, not wanting to lie directly.

"Take a letter," he said, and dictated a "Dear Sir, Yours Faithfully" type of boring official communication. I took notes as fast as I could, typed up the letter, partly from memory, and got the job.

After that, whenever I went into his office to take dictation, he would get me to sit opposite his desk, with my legs crossed and a notepad on my lap. And as he dictated some long, dull letter, he would seem to be scratching himself during the whole session. You can picture where. Being an innocent Jewish girl from Boston, I had no idea what he was really doing.

For the next year, I played at being secretary, but hated every minute of it. My so-called office was just a tiny dark wardrobe. But whenever the switchboard operator took a break or was absent, I took over her desk. I loved pulling out the plugs and putting them back into the holes on the switchboard and talking to people on the end of the line.

When there was a message to be delivered somewhere by hand, I made sure I was the delivery girl. I did everything I could to get out of my so-called office. For all this I received $50 a week. Good money, terrible job.

While I was working there, as well as altering the texts of letters, I managed to screw up the whole filing system. I would read the mail, and whenever a job application came in, I would start a new file in that name and put it away in alphabetical order. So of course, it was lost forever, unless someone went searching through all the files, name by name, opening each one up to see if it was a job application.

The best thing in that office was that I met a Polish refugee who was getting his medical degree in Boston, and we dated for a while. I thought we might be getting serious, but somehow my parents nixed the whole thing. I think they warned him off because they didn't want me to marry a Polish refugee.

Then in August, my boss told me he was going to spend a month in Israel, and he instructed me to read his mail while he was away. So, every day, I opened up his letters, read them and put them on his desk. All very routine.

When I came back from Labor Day Weekend, I was greeted at the door of the office by his old battle-axe secretary, the woman I had replaced, who had suddenly re-appeared in the office. She started screaming at me:

"Doctor Fineburg told you to read his mail!"

"I read it."

"Well you were supposed to write replies, letting people know he was out of town for the whole month of August!"

"He never told me that."

"Why do you think he told you to read his mail!?"

"I don't know. He didn't say."

"It didn't occur to you to let people know he wasn't reading his own mail!?"

"No. They might not have liked the idea that his secretary was reading everything. What if it was private?"

"You read his private letters?!"

"He told me to read everything." Though the most private thing he'd got all summer was a note from his doctor telling him he needed a check-up.

"You're fired!" she yelled.

I was shocked, and was going to defend myself, but then I realized that I really didn't want to go back to this stupid job with the boss who scratched himself at me. I was free again.

But free to do what?

Unfortunately, my parents had some ideas of their own.

Chapter 8

Is This What's *Meant* to Happen in the Marriage Bed?

I WAS SO INNOCENT BEFORE MARRIAGE. EVEN NOW, I FIND IT HARD to believe. Sometimes my innocence was just plain embarrassing. For example, when I was at college, everyone—men and women—had to go to a religious service at the chapel between 10 and 10:30 in the morning. The men usually sat on the pews on the right side of the aisle and the women on the left. Then one day the chaplain said he would like men and women to sit together. He gave us a little sermon about how fulfilling it would be for men and women to sit side by side, then he said, "And now we will all sing hymn number 69." And the whole class burst out laughing, except me.

I didn't dare ask anyone why they were laughing until the next day. I chose a girl I knew pretty well, who seemed much more mature than me, but who was kind. I knew she wouldn't laugh about my ignorance.

"What was so funny about hymn 69?" I asked her—out of everyone else's hearing, of course.

"You know...69," she said.

"No," I confessed. "What's funny about that?"

"Oh. Well, it implies oral sex."

"Why is that 69?" I wondered if this was something that had been invented in 1869, just after the Civil War. Or maybe in 1769, as one of the ways of breaking free of British colonial rule?

"The six and the nine are like the man and the woman doing it to each other."

I tried to imagine this: if the round parts of the six and the nine were the heads, this meant that one of the people was standing up, and the other was upside down. And both of them apparently had their face on their partner's feet? That wasn't how I imagined oral sex. Not that I'd imagined it very often.

"OK," I said, though I didn't really get what the two people were doing to each other. But I'm not sure she did, either.

IN PREPARATION FOR LIFE AFTER college, we all took a course called "Getting Ready for Marriage." Boy, did I need getting ready. I was still only necking, and I was now 21.

The course was always packed with bright-eyed women seniors. To give us an idea of how they thought they were saving our lives, the course was run by the college nurse. This was sex as medicine.

The course covered dating ("no French kissing"), sex before marriage ("no!"), and then instructed us how to be a good wife, which (at last!) included sex during marriage. Well, the very basics, anyway. The key message was, "Now you can let him do it."

At the end of the course, they gave us a little book with a test to take, listing a bunch of questions about a man that would tell us if he was marriage material. Does he open the door to allow you through first? Is he polite to your parents? Does he believe in God?

In my case, it really should have said, "Just sleep with the guy once, and ask yourself if this is the kind of disastrous marriage you want."

BACK HOME, CURED OF BEING a secretary, and primed for marriage, my father fixed me up with a blind date. One day another lawyer had walked into his office and said that he had a nice guy for me. His name was Seymore, and he was a Harvard graduate.

So, Seymore and I went on a date and I thought he was fine—he opened doors for me and was polite to my parents. Within two months, he asked me to marry him and gave me an engagement ring. I was very surprised and didn't know what to do. I didn't really want to marry the guy, and said I'd think about it.

Then one day Mom came screaming up the stairs to my room.

"I just talked to Seymore!" she yelled at me.

"Oh yes? Was he polite?"

"Polite? He's going crazy. Why won't you give him an answer?"

"Because I don't know how to say no politely."

"What? He wants to marry you! How many men want to marry you?"

"One, I guess."

"One is all you want! Well, one at a time. Marry him! You're 21 and still a spinster! Leave it much longer and no one will want you!"

All this was yelled at maximum volume so the whole neighborhood could hear. They were probably all choosing their outfits for the reception already.

But I wasn't giving in so easily. Marriage was for life, or so I'd been told. I wanted to be sure.

"You'll regret it!" Mom screamed, and she yelled her way back down the stairs again. I didn't know whether she meant I'd regret marriage or not getting married.

That Christmas, I went on a skiing vacation with Seymore (separate rooms, obviously), and he said that if we got married, we would go to Paris for our honeymoon. Call me superficial but that made up my mind. If the marriage was a disaster, at least I'd have Paris.

So NOW WE WERE ENGAGED, but still we didn't have sex. All we did was neck and pet for the seven months until the wedding date, that was set for July 28. Seymore seemed to want me to do more for him but he was too embarrassed to say what. Well, that suited me fine.

I still wasn't sure I wanted to marry him. I took out the marriage test from my college course and did the quiz. The results were clear: "Don't do it!" Had he told me he loved me? No! Did he tell me he missed me when we weren't together? No! Did he buy me flowers? No! Did he compliment me on the way I looked? Oh, come on, now you're just being absurd. The biggest compliment he ever paid anything was "That must have cost a lot of money."

But like a naïve fool I went ahead, and after the ceremony, we went to his parents' apartment, and all they could do was gloat about all the money that we got as gifts. We weren't leaving on our honeymoon till the next day, so we went to a motel in Boston, but it was 2 am and we were too tired to do anything but sleep. We didn't even kiss. Some wedding night that was.

As for the honeymoon, Seymore said we were going to Canada.

"What about Paris?" I asked.

"They speak French in Canada," he said.

"About ten people do, and they're all lumberjacks," I said. "I suppose you're going to say that Canada's pizza parlors are its Latin Quarter?"

"No, but I'm sure they have French restaurants."

So, I spent my honeymoon in Quebec instead of Paris. Not surprising that the sex turned out to be a pale imitation of the real thing, too. I read somewhere that "honeymoon" meant a month of sweetness, but all I got was a couple minutes of him grunting.

We drove all day and stopped off at a hotel in—believe it or not—Middlebury. I was going to lose my virginity in my college town, like so many Americans, but in my case a few years late.

We had a quick meal in the hotel dining room, then we went up to our room. I took off my clothes in the bathroom—I was still very shy—and put on a nightgown that Mom had chosen for me. It was long and heavy. "It'll keep you warm at night," she told me, as if she guessed Seymore was going to be a cold fish. Then I slipped into bed, where Seymore was waiting, smoking a cigarette, and wearing striped pajamas that looked as though he'd had them for years.

He put out the cigarette, which was polite of him, turned out the light, and then suddenly he was lying on top of me, poking around with his thumb (or so it felt). Then suddenly the thumb (or whatever it was) was inside me, and moving about while Seymore grunted, and I only just had time to think "Is this it?" before he made a noise like a guy who has just sunk a two-foot putt, and rolled off me again. I've had more fun riding a bicycle.

He kissed me once, which was polite of him, then fell asleep.

NEXT DAY, WE DROVE ON to a resort just north of Montreal, along roads that were like American highways, but with the occasional French name. Seymore had chosen a mountain resort, with a lake, tennis courts, and plenty of little black flies.

On our first day there, we met a charming French couple and played tennis with them. I partnered the husband at mixed doubles, and we got on great, with me chatting away in my best French—I even tried out one of Jean-Pierre's rude words when I missed a shot. Sadly, next day, the couple left. I think the French wife was scared her husband might try something on with me. He probably didn't know that he'd been chatting to a married woman who'd had sex only one time in her whole life.

Seymore and I saw plenty of other young couples at the resort who were holding hands, kissing and grabbing each other, as if they'd finally got permission to touch after months of waiting (which was probably true for most of them). Seymore and I wandered around like brother and sister, and talked about what we wanted from marriage—in his case, by the sound of it, regular meals and a house paid for by my grandparents. Then it was back to the hotel room for two minutes of grunting, which stretched out to three on the last night. I know because I'd started counting the seconds.

WHEN WE GOT BACK HOME, the sex didn't get any better. Every evening, Seymore would watch TV—hockey, football, or basketball. I would want to cuddle up, but he would only cuddle with me during the commercials. As soon as the game came on again, he would go back to watching it. Then in bed, before we went to sleep, he would make me masturbate him, and that that was the end of it. I was nothing more than the jerk jerking him off.

It got a little better on Saturdays, but not much. We would play touch football with the local kids in the park, or sometimes go to the tennis court. When we got home, he wanted to have sex, but never took a shower beforehand. He stank of sweat. Our sex life stank, period.

I WENT TO DIFFERENT MARRIAGE counselors, but Seymore wouldn't go because he was happy to keep doing the same old thing. One of the counselors, a woman, asked me the key question.

"How is the sex?"

Immediately I replied. "Is that all there is?"

She laughed. Not cruelly, I guess she'd just heard so many women say the same thing. I explained what was happening—or not happening—with Seymore.

"From what you tell me," she said, "I'd say your husband is not really keen on intercourse. He likes to be more passive. Why don't you try oral sex?"

"You mean 69?" I asked, though I wasn't keen on putting my face anywhere near his feet.

"Did you ever try oral sex before?" the marriage counselor asked. She seemed to know that I was still very ignorant about sex. At that time, I guess most of her female patients were.

"No," I admitted.

She explained what we could do, either simultaneously—nothing to do with feet, she assured me—or one after the other. I thought why not give it a try. Anything for a bit of pleasure.

I went home and told Seymore what she'd said. He knew I was going to marriage counselors, but he thought it was just so that someone could persuade me that everything about our relationship was normal.

"Oral sex?" he said. "And this was a woman counselor?" Maybe he thought only men knew about these things, or dared to talk about them.

"She said you might like it. And that I might enjoy getting it." Getting any enjoyment at all, I could have added.

"Nah," Seymore said. "I've never done it before. I don't really want to start."

It was a case of "Seymore, do less."

* * *

I WENT AND TOLD MY father that my marriage was a disaster. Of course, I couldn't talk about sex with him. But now I had other problems.

"He hit me," I said.

"Hit you?"

"Yes, he slapped my face when I told him I wasn't happy."

"Well don't tell him!" Dad said, though I could see that he was concerned. "A slap? Is that all?"

"Yes, it's not the first time. If I talk back to him, he slaps me. Or shakes me." I lifted my sleeve to show my father the bruises on my arms.

"Marriage isn't always easy," he said, and nodded towards the kitchen where Mom was preparing dinner. I knew what he meant. The screaming, the throwing things. And she'd given me more bruises than Seymore did. "But it's important," he added, and pointed to my wedding photo, which had pride of place on top of the television cabinet. "You have to work at it. You can't just give up."

"I could ask for a divorce," I said.

"No, no, divorce is a painful, messy business." He'd dealt with hundreds of divorce cases during his career.

"Less messy than my marriage," I said.

But he just shook his head. "Work at it. You'll get used to each other."

Even then, I guessed that what he meant was that he didn't want a divorcee daughter.

Back in conservative early 60s America, divorce was still shameful, unless you were a Hollywood star. The mess he talked about didn't refer to what would happen to me, it was the endless gossip that he and Mom would have to put up with.[1]

Sexually, my marriage wasn't an entire waste of time, though this wasn't really thanks to Seymore.

I got an awakening of sorts on a trip to Provincetown, on the tip of Cape Cod. Even then, it was the gay capital of the northeast–though most Bostonians didn't know a thing about it. Seymore and I stayed for a long weekend at a bed and breakfast, and we noticed that the town was full of all these guys dressed in flamboyant shirts, wearing gold chains around their necks, happily hanging out together.

I whispered to Seymore, "I think those men are ho-mo-sex-uals ..." (The word "gay" hadn't been invented yet.)

He said: "No, no, no, they're just guys who are dressed up for the beach."

At dinner that night, I mustered up my innocent courage and talked to an older man in the restaurant who was wearing one of those loud-and-proud shirts.

"Are you guys ho-mo-sex-uals ...?" I asked him.

He leaned in close and said: "Yes, we are." He was so kind. "If you really want to see the young ones in action, go to the dunes tomorrow morning."

---

[1] This was confirmed for me two years after my divorce, when I came home from Paris and saw that my parents still had my wedding picture on top of the television cabinet. They had never told anybody that I was a divorced woman.

Surprisingly, Seymore was interested. Maybe, like me, he had some repressed urges going on. So next morning, we were up bright and early, and we went to the dunes and spread out our blanket to wait for the show.

A group of four guys came to the foot of the nearest dune, and set up camp. Disappointingly, though, they weren't camp at all. They were acting just like conventional American males—laughing, sunbathing, talking about their girlfriends.

"She talked to that guy, and I swear she was flirting so much, and do you *know* what she said to him?" It was boring, like girl talk from college. But then one of them stood up and had a big old hissy fit.

"She was drunk last night! *So* drunk!" he shouted. "She couldn't even walk. I was *so* embarrassed!" And while he was saying all this, he kept pointing to the GUY sitting right next to him. Seymore and I looked at each other with utter amazement! Oh my God, the "she's" they were discussing were really "he's". They *were* homosexuals!

That night we kept our eyes peeled. We went to *all* the bars, saw all the men talking, dancing, and making out in the shadowy corners. For two innocents from Boston, this was a huge awakening.

So far, though, for me it was all just spectator sport, and seemed to concern males only.

However, that same evening, I did have a more personal enlightenment. As we strolled through the streets of Provincetown, back to our bed and breakfast, we found ourselves walking behind two women. And they were holding hands, like lovers. I had never seen two women do that. I found myself paying more attention to them than to Seymore, who was saying that he thought ho-mo-sexuals were, on the whole, "unnatural." He kept repeating that word.

Meanwhile, I stared and stared at the two women, and became curious, and a little jealous, too. Their holding hands seemed to be the most natural thing in the world.

For the moment, though, I didn't know what to do about these feelings. I didn't wonder if I would ever get to the stage of holding hands with another woman. So far, I was stuck in a "normal" marriage to a man whose sexual appetites seemed a lot more "unnatural" than the men we'd seen in the dunes. At least those guys openly showed that they cared about each other.

THE NEXT TIME I SAW my mother, I told her all about these homosexuals we'd seen, and put my pantomime skills to work showing her how the guys walked the streets, with their hips swaying and their arms sashaying around. She watched me and said:

"Oh, Diana, that's the way *you* should be walking."

"What?"

"Yes. Copy them! Swing your hips, bend your elbows!"

"Thanks, Mom. The recipe for saving my marriage is to act like a homosexual guy?"

"Exactly!"

Well, with hindsight, maybe she was right.

SEYMORE AND I FUMBLED ALONG for another three years. I never *quite* admitted it to myself, but I think I may have fancied his sister more than him.

In the end I decided to get a lawyer. Not my father, because he would have done all he could to stop the divorce. Besides, he refused to handle the case, and kept telling me that deep down Seymore was a good man. So in the end, I found myself another attorney, and to be fair, Dad offered to pay the fees.

The attorney was very matter-of-fact.

"Do you have a lot of shared assets?" he wanted to know. Maybe so that I could pay his bills. "Do you own a house together?"

"No, we rent." I explained that we were *supposed* to have bought a house. After I told my father that I was unhappy, my grandfather had given us $20,000 to buy a home and solidify the marriage. But we'd never spent it. Seymore had said we should leave it in the bank. A joint account, naturally.

"That's your money," my lawyer told me. "Take it out of the joint account before your husband knows you're leaving him. Otherwise he'll take it all."

"He'd never do that!" I said.

But my lawyer told me I couldn't be too careful, so I took the money out, went back home to my parents, and left Seymore a note saying that if he agreed to marriage counseling, I would go back to him. Next day, he called me. He sounded worried, which was satisfying.

"Diana, you've really left me?"

"Yes. Without counseling, it's not going to work."

"I see."

"You do? That's promising, at least."

"Er, Diana?"

"Yes?"

"Did you take the money out of our joint account?"

"Yes, I took *my* money back."

"It was in a joint account, so it was *our* money."

"It was a gift from my grandfather to try and save our marriage. You didn't want to spend it on saving our marriage, so I took it back."

"I'm going to sue you."

"That's all you've got to say?"

"I'm going to sue you and get the money back."

"Oh, thanks, that's much better."

End of marriage.

THE DIVORCE WAS GRANTED AFTER I promised to give him back all the wedding gifts his family had given me, as well as the diamond engagement ring, and $2,000.

When it had all been settled, my brother Herbie called to console me.

"You were right to leave him," he said.

I knew that, but asked him why.

"I just found out from my father-in-law, before you got married, Seymore's parents asked them how much money grandfather had. You see what kind of people they were?"

Even if I was relieved to be divorced, this came as a shock. So Seymore had only married me for my money, and not for my body, my smile, my wit and charm? Not even for sex? My expectations had been low, but hell!

Still, even if my divorce took away most of my self-esteem, I still had $18,000. And a great idea how to spend it.

My first baby picture, and disobeying the rules for the time. "Look at the camera," they told me.

MUSIC ENRICHES LIFE...

My first advertisement—for a music school. I was about seven, and hoping that one day I'd reach the pedals on my piano.

Age seven at camp in
New Hampshire, where
I learned to swim topless.
Later I learned to swim
in a full bathing costume.

Front row, right. I was the catcher of the junior high softball team until
a ball hit me in the mouth.

When I was a teenager, my mother thought that photographing me near books would make me look more intelligent.

As swimming counselor at a camp near Boston. As far as I know, none of the girls drowned.

Second from right. When I was 16, I thought life would always be about sitting on a Mexican exchange student's knee.

Fooling around at girls' camp. It would be years before anyone else asked me to take my bra off.

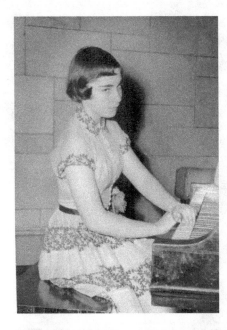

When I was about 20, I started to cultivate my mysterious French cabaret artiste look.

THE MIDDLEBURY COLLEGE CHOIR

The director of my college choir told me, "Don't tell anyone, but I'm Jewish too."

College graduation with my parents. I got a BA with Honors and a walking stick.

My wedding in 1958, looking happy because I didn't know what was yet to come.

DIANA LUNN

*Dramatic Soprano
and
Monologist*

*A Versatile, Talented, and
Refreshing Entertainer*

Contact: HARRY WALKER, *Agent*
100 Boylston St., Boston, Mass.
HAncock 6-2334

My first publicity brochure. One of my "mon-
ologues" involved me doing a striptease, in
pantomime.

Chapter 9

I'll Always Have Paris

FOR THE NEXT TWO YEARS, I HAD A BALL IN PARIS, AND experienced everything the city had to offer. And I mean *everything*. I thought that for once it was lucky I wasn't a WASPy Christian, because it was all pure sin.

Officially, I was there to study French and mime. But of course, that wasn't the only kind of French bodily movement I was keen to learn. I was 29 years old, practically a virgin, and dying to broaden my horizons.

I had booked myself into the Lutèce, the hotel where the returning Jewish refugees had been housed immediately after the War. In my own way, I was a returning refugee too. But this was a really fancy place, and I quickly realized that I was going to spend all my money in a week or so if I stayed there, so I found a cheap but horribly noisy hotel at Odéon, and then an even cheaper shared apartment near Montparnasse. It would have been the ideal situation to help me improve my French, except that my two roommates were the first ever French people I'd known who didn't want to talk to me.

I signed up for a course at the Sorbonne, in French language and phonetics. It sounded like an essential education for a visitor like me—until I went to the first lesson.

In a gigantic amphitheater, with maybe 400 other students, most of them much younger than me, and in groups of friends, an ancient-looking professor talked for an hour about the importance of obeying the rules of French grammar and spelling. Unwelcome news for someone like me who'd come to Paris to break all the rules. These were historic rules, he said, and existed for a reason, and that reason was that they were to be obeyed. He sounded like a judge, just before he sentences you to ten years in jail. The aim was perfection, and nothing less was acceptable. All in all, I preferred Jean-Pierre's method of teaching—"here's a really vulgar word, try to pronounce it."

I stuck with the Sorbonne course for a while, but it didn't teach me anything about French except that you can argue for an hour about whether a word should end in an E or not, and that it's really important to learn tenses that no one uses anymore, *ever*.

All very fascinating and historical, I'm sure, but not that useful when you're trying to have a chat in a bar. Maybe that's why my roommates didn't talk to me. I must have sounded like Marie-Antoinette.

Finally, after a lot of begging on my part to the university, I got a room at Paris' main student residence on the southern edge of the city, the Cité Universitaire, and suddenly my social life really took off.

My room was tiny and purely functional—bed, desk, chair, lamp, bookshelf—but as soon as I arrived with my suitcase, a friendly face popped out of the room next door. She was a Spanish girl who had been living there for a few months. She told me that the Cité Universitaire was a wonderful place to live and meet people, but you had to obey some essential ground rules. It sounded like French grammar all over again, but we went to the cafeteria and she explained over an incredibly cheap coffee.

"Don't get carried away with the sociability: whatever you do, don't go to the rooms of any of the guys who invite you to come up for 'a cup of tea'."

"You mean, it's not only the drink that's going to be hot?" To me, it sounded quite exciting.

"Exactly. A girl was raped here a couple months ago."

Not so exciting. What a great start to my Parisian adventure—the choice between no sex and rape. Less romantic than I'd hoped.

I decided I needed to keep studying, so I looked around for a singing teacher. I went to the *conservatoire*, the public music school where all France's best musicians are trained, and asked about lessons. It sounded as though I couldn't sign up at the conservatoire without getting a French passport and sitting three years of exams, but they recommended a teacher.

I got all dressed up and went to her apartment. She lived in an ancient building with a palatial stone staircase, and her apartment was decorated with antique vases and statues, with gilded drapes and exquisite paintings all over the place. I had never seen anything like it in my life.

She had me sing a song for her—I chose one of the classical-sounding hymns I'd sung at college—and she said that I had potential.

"When would you like to start lessons?" she asked.

"As soon as possible," I said.

"How about Monday at ten?"

"Oh no, first I have to see a few other teachers, so I can decide who's best for me."

This was the typical American attitude. I'm going to be paying, so I want the best service possible.

"I see," she said, and was suddenly less complimentary about my potential.

The *conservatoire* called me the next day and told me that the teacher was highly insulted, and that she would never teach me even if I chose her. I'd learnt an important lesson: in France, everyone in the arts thinks they're a major star. So you, humble student, don't decide if you want to hire a singing teacher. They decide they want to teach you, and you're incredibly lucky that they've granted you the opportunity to share their genius when they could be filling the opera every night with adoring crowds (in their dreams, of course).

I was very upset, because I didn't want to insult anyone. The school gave me the name of a teacher called Monsieur Derenne. Determined not to commit any more diplomatic gaffes, I set off next morning.

He lived right opposite a métro station in the western suburb of Neuilly (pronounced something like "no-yee"). The building was relatively fancy, but it was on the main road into town. I wondered how I'd hear myself sing. Then again, it would be good practice at increasing the volume of my voice.

Desperate to succeed with my second attempt at getting a teacher, I sang my hymn again. He nodded, looked satisfied.

"Would you possibly accept me as a student?" I asked. I'd learnt the right attitude now.

"Yes, I would be delighted. But...." He looked at me nervously. "Will you be interviewing other teachers?"

I almost had to laugh. The school had evidently warned him about this pushy American. I'd sent a wave of terror through the Parisian music-teaching community.

I immediately reassured him.

"I would love to come for lessons with you," I told him, and he gave me a huge smile.

I started to go and sing with Monsieur Derenne every week, and he was a charming, encouraging teacher. The only problem was that we studied French art songs—what they call *chansons françaises*. The French love them, because they have complicated, witty lyrics, but most of them have repetitive melodies that you could never hum without someone thinking you were moaning about toothache. I like a good tune that you can remember and sing to yourself, but Monsieur Derenne's favorite *chansons* were as memorable as a rainy day in Maine. But at least he was training my voice and teaching me a lot more French. With those *chansons françaises*, you have to position your vowels exactly right.

As well as trying to make more noise, I was also studying how to be silent. I'd signed up for a course at the famous Jacques Lecoq school of mime, with the famous Monsieur Lecoq himself.

Ironically for a mime teacher, he had a very loud voice, and if I got something wrong, he'd bellow like a bear with indigestion. Also, he had an incredibly expressive face, but often covered it up with an expressionless white mask. He had long spiky hair, and big, mobile features, making him almost ugly but he had charisma by the barrelful.

He taught me the basics of mime, which seemed to be using invisible props. (I don't know why the school was so expensive—they didn't exactly need much equipment.) I learned to pretend that I was holding a pole or stick (of different sizes), that I couldn't carry a heavy suitcase, piles of books, rock or whatever (though I never understood why I would be carrying a rock), that I was trying to pull something along on the end of a rope (the suitcase, maybe?), and of course that I was stuck inside a box or behind an invisible wall. Though I've never understood who gets themselves stuck behind an invisible wall. Except flies, maybe, but all they do is headbutt the window.

I was disappointed that we didn't mime a striptease. I'd have loved to perfect my sketch but removing clothes wasn't on the syllabus. Removing stuff that had got stuck to your hands, yes. I don't know how many hours I spent pretending I had sticky palms or fingers. I can mime any type of glue you could name.

The most important thing for me was that I was learning to move, and feel comfortable in my body. I've never used mime in my singing or comedy acts. I'm someone who loves to make noise, to use words and melodies to get a reaction from the audience. But I guess Jacques Lecoq did teach me to use my face, my eyes and my body to express myself while I'm talking or singing. Though I'm not sure he would have approved of playing *everything* for laughs. Those French mime artists were really serious about their art.

On my way to and from classes at the mime school, I learned almost as much as during lessons. Classes began at 8 am, and I was always astonished to walk past the cafés at that time in the morning and see Frenchmen propping up against the bar, drinking glasses of wine or beer. These weren't bums, they were often well-dressed, wearing work overalls or a suit, and carrying briefcases. A quick shot of alcohol before work seemed to be the norm, unlike in Boston where we had strict laws against early morning boozing. I even used to see one man come out of the café, wobbling slightly, and walk into the nearby school. Though I can imagine that with some difficult schoolkids, it's best to arrive in class drunk. The strange thing was that I hardly ever saw Parisian women boozing before work. Maybe they waited until afterwards.

On my way home, I sometimes used to wander past the *bouquinistes* by the Seine, the tiny book stalls that are bolted to the walls along the riverside, and that fold out to reveal their treasures. To a young Bostonian, these were thrilling places. Back home, any book that was a little sexy was banned. (I'm sure the good citizens of Boston would have banned a few books in the bible, if they'd actually read them all.) But Paris was famous as a place where anything went, publishing wise, so the *bouquinistes* used to stock everything racy for the tourists. I bought the Marquis de Sade, for example. I had to use a dictionary to understand a lot of the words, and quickly realized that he was a real sicko. It was titillating at first, because he just listed one sexual act after the other—"so and so did this, then that, with him, then her, with his hand, his mouth, then his...." You get the picture. But after a while it was just boring (if that's not a bad pun.)

Sometimes the *bouquinistes* had banned books in English, too. I read *Lady Chatterley's Lover*, which was much more erotic than Sade. I got the hots for Lady Chatterley—she was one sexy lady. I read Henry Miller, and could identify with him. He was like a kid who'd just arrived in an all-you-can-eat ice cream store. He wrote as if sex didn't even exist in America. Well, in marriages like mine, he was right.

All in all, I was getting a fantastic all-round education in the arts.

TO MEET PEOPLE WHO DIDN'T want to mime at me, I also joined Four Winds, an international adventure club where everyone talked about their travel experiences. There, I got talking to a pleasant guy who didn't seem to be the type to invite a girl for "tea." He was tall and dark-haired, with a well-trimmed beard. He had a bit of an accent when he spoke French. But then, so did I.

"Where are you from?" he asked me.

"America," I said, quite flattered that he had to ask. Most people in France can spot an American accent as if we were wearing the Star-spangled Banner tattooed on our face. "What about you?"

"Austria," he said. I gulped. Obviously, given my background, I was a little wary of German speakers. I couldn't stop myself wondering whether they wouldn't try to turn me into a lampshade. "I'm from Graz, near the Yugoslav border." That sounded a little better—the Yugoslavs had been on the Allied side, right? "I'm an engineer, working for the French government," he went on. "I live in Rambouillet."

"Rom-boo-yay?"

We had some fun pronouncing this in our different accents, and he told me that Rambouillet, just southwest of Paris, was where De Gaulle had stopped for a quick rest in 1944 before liberating the city (with the help of a few Americans, though Parisians often seem to forget that). The Austrian, who said his name was Gerhard, didn't sound upset that Paris had been liberated, so that was reassuring. And he was very charming and soft-spoken, so I accepted his invitation to go out on a lunch date.

The following Sunday, he picked me up at the Cité Universitaire in his car—I didn't realize then that men with cars were something of a rarity in Paris—and drove me out to a country restaurant. I have no idea where it was. I just enjoyed the drive with this charming, funny man who seemed to take an interest in me. The exact opposite of my ex-husband.

For the first time in my life, I ate tiny crawfish shells, and Gerhard showed me how to pull them apart with my fingers. And he said it was perfectly acceptable to let the juice run down my chin. It was all so erotic.

Of course, after a lunch like that, I went back to his apartment—which just happened to be very close to the restaurant. Gerhard was an engineer, remember, skilled at technical details. And there, he showed me that his fingers were good at a lot more than shelling crawfish. Other parts of him were pretty gifted too. He was very gentle, and told me that he knew how to satisfy a woman. He wasn't exaggerating. He took me in hand (in more ways than one), and in one afternoon, and the following night, he gave me a complete sexual education. And to think that I'd been married and missed out on all these delights with Seymore "what's a clitoris?" Cohen.

After that, he asked me to come and spend the night at least twice a week. So, I used to take the evening train out of Paris with the returning commuters. Occasionally, we would meet on the weekend in a hotel at Montparnasse. I was living my Parisian dream.

I NOW HAD MY FIRST French boyfriend, and he was an Austrian. Nobody's perfect. Though Gerhard very nearly was. Like me, he loved to sing, and he even got me crooning in German. Whenever we said goodbye, we'd sing the old Marlene Dietrich song, "Lili Marlene". OK, it's about a whore who hangs around in front of an army barracks, but like I said, nobody's perfect. Also, that line about her standing "underneath a lantern" kind of reminded me of lampshades, but hell, I was in love.

My mother came to Paris for a visit.

I met up with her near her hotel in the Opéra neighborhood of Paris. We sat in a café, in back, where we had more chance of a private conversation. Because of Mom's hearing problems, conversations with her very rarely private.

"You're living in a student room?" she half-yelled. She made it sound like prison. "Come back to Boston."

"Why, Ma? I'm enjoying myself here." I didn't tell her exactly how.

"Come back and marry a nice Jewish man."

"But Ma...."

"Well, he doesn't have to be nice. Or Jewish. Just marry *someone*. You're almost thirty. You can't be a *divorcee* living like a *student*."

"But I'm happy, Ma!"

"What's that got to do with it? It's much better to be married than happy."

I told her I'd think about it and offered to walk her around the neighborhood. And there, right by the Opéra, we bumped into Gerhard. I introduced him to Mom. I'd already told him stories about her hearing, so he mouthed his name very clearly.

"Gerhard Schneider?" she repeated. "Sounds almost Jewish."

He was so charming and polite that she loved him instantly, and after he left, she told me: "Marry him!"

"But Ma, he's Austrian. What if his uncles were Nazis?"

"Nazis, Schmazis. You're single, and you're over 25. Marry him!"

I SERIOUSLY BEGAN TO THINK about it. I wondered if Gerhard would stay in Paris, or want to return to Austria. And either way, what would I do to earn a living? I didn't want to be a Hausfrau. I wondered if he'd want to come to America. We needed engineers, right? And hadn't we imported lots of Germans after the war to work on our nuclear programs?

But then one day, not long after meeting my mother, Gerhard told me he was going back home to Austria—to marry his fiancée. This Fraülein was a little detail he had neglected to mention to me or my mother.

It came as a shock, and something of a disappointment, but deep down I felt that it was for the best. Gerhard had taught me all he knew, and now I was ready to move on. I knew that Paris had a lot more to offer.

Chapter 10

Hooking up with a Hooker

I WENT TO LIVE WITH MY FRIEND, MADO, WHO IS STILL ONE OF my dearest friends. She lived near Pigalle, and being French, she was far more experienced than I could ever be. She was sleeping with the local Catholic priest.[2]

I'd been to Pigalle before, and seen the streetwalkers, so I knew it was sleazy. But it was also fun. It was like the old Edith Piaf song, "Milord." And Piaf was still alive, by the way, and still singing that song. (She died while I was in Paris, in October 1963, and the French mourned as much as we did for JFK, who died a month later.)

Now I had more time to watch the Parisian prostitutes flirting with the male tourists. I realized that these women standing in every doorway were the most outrageous human beings I'd ever seen. Some of them wore fur coats with nothing else underneath, except high-heeled shoes. Whether they were 20 years old or 60, they had hair dyed blonder than Marilyn Monroe, and their lips were redder than ripe strawberries.

---

[2] One might be forgiven for thinking, "the local Catholic priest was sleeping with an *adult woman*?"

The men would wander around, not-so-discreetly eying up the ladies of the night (or afternoon, or morning), who touted openly for business, calling out in English, "Come wiz me, Milord, come wiz me!" And plenty of the "lords" would come *wiz zem*.

Mado told me that some of the girls preferred the morning shift—at least the clients had probably just showered. Lots of French guys would go and see a hooker on their way to work. Kind of the equivalent of joggers these days. Later in the day, or at night, those same guys would smell a whole lot less fresh. Not like lords at all.

Pretty soon, I had my own first brush with a hooker. Well, it was a lot more than a brush.

TO BROADEN MY HORIZONS, I went to a club near Montparnasse that I'd heard about. It was called Elle et Lui, and it was divided into two sections. One put on shows for women (Elle) and the other was aimed towards men (Lui).

It was in a small side street just off the main boulevard, hidden away, but close to the big fashionable cafés. I could imagine people having dinner in one of the brasseries, then heading to Elle et Lui for some late-evening fun.

I turned up at 10pm, opening time, and of course it was practically empty. I went into the women's section, and saw a few boyishly dressed girls, like the ones I'd spotted walking around in Saint-Germain. These girls were just standing around staring at each other or talking to the "*entraîneuse*" (the female "trainer" whose job was to encourage clients to drink).

I sat at the bar and ordered a ginger ale that cost 15 Francs, a fortune at the time. But then one of my father's more useful pieces of advice had been: "Always be prepared to be cheated in a nightclub." I sipped it slowly and watched couples arriving—mainly female couples. This was getting interesting.

After an hour, my ginger ale was all gone, but I didn't want to leave, so I ordered another. (That was when I learned the French trick at the time in nightclubs—buy a cognac and make it last all evening. I've been using it ever since.)

At last, a woman asked me to dance. She was cute, blonde, and German. I wondered what it was with these Austrians and Germans, going for the Jewish girl.

We danced till about 2 am, laughing and chatting, then doing a romantic cheek to cheek. It felt very natural, but at the same time it was unbelievably new and exciting to me. I realized I'd been dreaming of doing this ever since I saw those two women holding hands in Provincetown maybe four or five years earlier.

I asked my new German friend if she wanted to meet up in a café after the club closed, and she said yes, but then she came back and told me that she was going home with a couple she'd danced with earlier. Two for the price of one. I couldn't compete.

But I didn't get discouraged. I went back to the club on another night and bought myself a cognac. But this time no one seemed interested. I didn't dance at all. Finally, someone came over, but it was a guy.

"You don't look as though you're having fun," he said.

"No," I agreed.

"Why did you come here?" he asked. He wasn't being aggressive. He really wanted to know. I decided to be straight with him.

"I just got divorced, and I've never been with a woman, so I thought I'd like to try it. But I'm not having much luck."

"I know a woman who would be interested," he told me.

"You do?" Suddenly my boring evening had come alive.

"If I can join in."

He looked like a pretty clean-living guy, fairly attractive. And he was providing the entertainment, so I thought, why not? We got in his car and drove over to an apartment building near the Arc de Triomphe. It was a chic building with a big, clunky iron elevator. Old-school Paris.

On the fourth or fifth floor, we were greeted by a friendly, glamorous-looking woman who invited us into her apartment, offered us a drink, and then invited us to get it on. Simple as that.

"Who wants to start?" she asked, unzipping her dress already.

The guy asked me if I minded him going first, and I said be my guest. Or rather her guest.

We all went into the bedroom, and I sat and watched him making love with her, pretty conventionally. A lot less slow and gentle than Gerhard had been, but the woman didn't seem to mind. Then, when he'd finished, he got off the bed and lit a cigarette, and motioned me to take his place. And I did. A sexy, glamorous Parisian woman and me, doing new things, some of them shocking to me, some of them just exciting, but all of them very educational. A lot more so than anything I had learned at the Sorbonne.

* * *

So now I had lost my gay virginity and I wanted more. One afternoon, on my own, I went back to the Arc de Triomphe neighborhood and found the woman's apartment. But when she opened the door, she looked shocked and said she wasn't interested.

"But the other night, it was fun," I said.

"It was business," she answered. "Your friend paid for your evening's entertainment."

"How much was it?" I asked.

She told me—about the same as a month's rent at the Cité Universitaire. I thought maybe I should have charged him, too—he had got me for free.

STILL, BEING WITH TWO PEOPLE in one night had opened my eyes to even greater possibilities, and pretty soon I got my chance to explore them.

One evening I was sitting in the Café Select in Montparnasse when a smooth Frenchman started talking to me. The usual at first:

"Bonsoir, Mademoiselle, may I join you? My name is Jacques (or Pierre or François, or whatever), what is yours? Oh, such a pretty name! And I love your accent, it is so *charmant*." So far, so unsurprising, but then, within ten minutes of meeting me, he invited me to a party in a chic neighborhood of Paris, the Seventh *arrondissement*. I knew this was very fancy. There are government ministries in the Seventh, the prime minister's palace (yes, they have one palace for the president, and another for the prime minister), and some very big mansions they call "*hôtels particuliers*"— private hotels.

As soon as the guy got me alone in the taxi, I understood that his party wasn't going to be a fancy reception with the prime minister.

"There will be dancing," he said, "and something else... something *très sexy*."

And his fingers began to dance up my legs and underneath my skirt. I slapped his hand. But he just smiled. He knew what was coming next.

We arrived at a big house—an "*hôtel particulier*," very chic, and walked through a beautiful garden. In the house, two very sexy women told us to give them all of our clothes.

"Our clothes? Do you mean our coats?" I asked.

"Your clothes! You must be naked!"

I told them, "No thank you, I grew up in Boston. In Boston, at parties, we keep our clothes on. Even when we have sex, we wear our pajamas."

But the women were insistent: "Vous devez dérober!" You have to get undressed!

I thought, oh well, when in Paris....

After "dérobeying," I went into the next room and sat on the corner of a huge bed. There were maybe 30 or 40 people there—with no clothes on. It was so civilized, everyone joking, laughing, talking—but all stark naked. Then discreetly, and not so discreetly, they began making moves on each other. I was shocked. I mean, at the Arc de Triomphe, it had been just three of us, pretty intimate. But here at the party, it was a whole naked crowd. It was like getting it on in the public library. (I've had nightmares exactly like that.)

I watched for a while, cringing, but gradually, seeing them all get down to it, I got curious, and slowly... very slowly... I moved closer, and I joined in. I got it on with a man, then a woman, then apparently everyone at the same time.

Yes, I started swinging. And that night in the chic Seventh *arrondissement* of Paris, with all the different combinations that were going on, I became a new woman....

A really happy woman.

Inevitably, though, it was too good to be true. My satisfaction was a bubble, waiting to burst. A champagne bubble about to lose its fizz.

Chapter 11

Dragged Back to Boston...

ALL THIS TIME, MY PARENTS WERE CONTACTING ME, TELLING ME to come home to Boston and get married. They even convinced my old marriage counselor to get in touch and warn me that if I didn't come home and find a husband, I was going to turn into a lesbian. (How did she guess what I was getting up to in Paris?)

In the end, my mother came back to Paris and virtually dragged me back to Boston where I quickly realized that if I stayed there and looked for a husband, I was going to go nuts. After anything-goes Paris, it felt like prison. In France, I'd been to nightclubs where women danced with women and men hooked you up with hookers. In Boston, people fainted if a Catholic went on a date with a Jew.

WHICH REMINDS ME OF ONE thing that happened around this time. It was the twist in the tail of my European family's history.

When my dear old grandfather died in 1963, we found out that he had left $10,000 in his will to a cousin in Latvia. This was news to us—another survivor of the war?

My grandfather had apparently been convinced that she was alive and he wanted her to come to the USA to find safety. The condition in his will was that she would get the money if she came to fetch it in person.

A friend of my father's was a lawyer who worked with the Soviet Government and he managed to find my cousin living in Latvia, which was then part of the USSR. Amazingly, the Soviets allowed her to come to America to get the money. I guess they threatened her family with reprisals if she didn't go straight back afterwards and give them a share.

So, she came over, and stayed with my parents. I went to meet her, and when I walked into the room, I got a shock. Yetta Kramer looked like my mother. There were differences: she was wearing a Soviet dress that seemed to be made out of radioactive nylon. It almost seemed to buzz when she moved. Her shoes were a model that went out of date in Boston in about 1880. And she had a little beard running across her chin. Dozens of little hairs about quarter of an inch long. They obviously didn't have electrolysis in Soviet Russia. Or mirrors.

Yetta didn't speak any English, but my father managed to speak with her in Yiddish. Through him, I asked Yetta how she survived the war. She nodded sadly and spoke a couple of short sentences. Dad translated.

"She escaped into the forest and was able to live there until Latvia was liberated."

We waited for more details, but she didn't give any. It was obviously a painful subject. Even so, I wish I had asked more questions. This was the first person I had met who had survived that horrific time. It would have been so interesting to hear what went on in Nazi-occupied countries from the victims' point of view. It was around then that I started thinking about going to visit a concentration camp in Germany, Poland, or one of the other occupied countries. I started to feel the need to investigate the workings of the regime that wanted to exterminate people like Yetta and me. It would be a few more years before I was able to put the idea into practice.

Quite a few uncles, aunts and cousins came to see Yetta, and some of them talked to her in Yiddish. We found out that she was sharing an apartment with four other families, and could hardly believe that we had empty rooms in our houses. We fed her on American food, and when she ate strawberries from our garden, she almost cried. She told Dad she hadn't tasted them since she was a young woman, before the war, before all the different invasions of Latvia.

After a few days with her American family, Yetta went back to Latvia. I just hope she got to keep some of the $10,000.

NO ONE WAS GIVING ME free money at this time, so I went into teaching. I'd done this while I was married, teaching sports and biology in Boston. Not much fun, but it was something I could do. (And back then, there had certainly been a lot more sporting activity and biology in my lessons that in my marital bed.)

When I came back from Paris in 1964, I decided to go back into education. An easy way to make a living, I thought.

But I was wrong. The guy who interviewed me for a job in the Boston school system was not at all impressed by my résumé. He started down at it through thick eyeglasses.

"You spent two whole years in Paris studying mime?" he asked.

"I took lessons in opera singing too."

He stared at me as if I was crazy. Or a bit perverted.

"Didn't you study any French?"

"Well, yes, I started a course at the Sorbonne, but it was so old-fashioned."

"Old-fashioned? Of course, it was! The Sorbonne is one of the world's oldest universities! And you left there to study mime?" He made me feel as if I'd been caught doing a strip-tease in the Vatican.

"And opera," I reminded him.

"What a frivolous waste of time," he said.

Lucky, I didn't tell him about the other kind of education I'd been getting in Paris.

This guy thought I wasn't serious-minded enough to be a teacher so I had to fall back on the classic "it's who you know" technique, just as I had done (unknowingly) to get into college... my father knew a judge who knew someone in education who got me a job at the Horace Mann School for the Deaf in Roxbury, the neighborhood where I grew up.

Horace Mann was a strange place. It didn't teach the students sign language, the idea being that they would fit into society more if they were forced to learn how to read lips. This wasn't very liberal, but then it was an institution with an Irish Catholic principal. Even so, kids being kids, they found a way round the problem—they developed their own unique sign language that nobody else could understand. How to beat the system. I admired them for it.

I had a pretty weird job. First, I had to teach basketball to hearing-impaired teenage boys. Yes, a five-foot-tall woman teaching basketball. They were pretty good, and we went to play against all sorts of regular schools, and we often won.

I also taught the boys biology—starting with plants and animals. Inevitably, there was a chapter in the book about animal reproduction. And I don't just mean queen bees laying eggs. When we got to the section about mammals, I could see the boys start to sign to each other in class. Here was something that interested them a lot more than plants.

One of the boys raised his hand, while others started giggling or looking embarrassed. I could tell what was coming.

"Yes?"

He spoke in his slightly slurred accent, moving his lips really clearly so his classmates could understand.

"How do people reproduce?"

Well, at least it was a straight question. I wondered how to answer.

After my time in Paris, I knew a lot more about this than when I was married. But I was acutely conscious that I had to stay within the bounds of teaching a school biology class. I would have to stick to the biological basics, and steer clear of actual pleasure. Which was a shame. After all, birds do it, bees do it, even educated fleas do it, so why shouldn't you talk about it frankly and openly in the education system?

"Just like the diagram in your book," I said. There was a line drawing of male and female reproductive organs that could have represented machine parts. There was no sign of erection or excitement or ejaculation.

"But what actually happens between a man and a woman?" the boy asked, and his classmates were all staring at me expectantly.

Poor kids, I thought. They were 16, but they knew absolutely nothing. I realized that most kids learn about sex by talking among themselves, *sotto voce*. But these kids couldn't hear anything *sotto voce*, or even *voce*.

So, I tried to answer by describing, as coldly and clearly as possible, what went on. The male part went inside the female part, then the semen squirts into the uterus....

"Straight away?" the brave kid asked.

Again, this wasn't a provocative question, as it almost certainly would have been with a bunch of kids with good hearing. They really wanted to know.

"Not straight away," I said. "It can take a few minutes." With Seymore, very few.

"Without moving?"

"No, the male usually goes in and out." With Gerhard, I thought, in and out, in and out....

"What does it feel like?" Now we were going too far.

"I wouldn't know, I'm not male." They groaned, and signed to each other again. They wanted their spokesman to press on with his questions. "That's enough," I told them. "Let's return to the books. Mammals...."

I thought I'd managed to handle a tricky situation pretty well. After all, a classroom full of young male virgins was a volcano of hormones. I'd kept the lid on and prevented an eruption, hadn't I?

However, a couple of weeks later, when I entered the school one morning, Miss Denehy, the principal, told me to come directly to her office.

She went and sat behind her desk, and didn't invite me to sit down.

"I hear you're teaching sex," she said. She grimaced as if the word left a bad taste in her mouth. Though I didn't think she'd ever done anything remotely sexy with that tight-lipped orifice.

"No, I taught animal reproduction, as it's described in the school textbook."

"But you described human reproduction."

"Humans are animals, aren't they?" She gave me a look that suggested I definitely was an animal.

"You know it's against the law in Boston to teach anything in school about sex."

I didn't like to ask how the city's Catholics had so many children without knowing about sex, so I just promised I would stay away from the subject for the rest of the year (in my lessons, at least).

But when I went into class that day, the boys started raising their hands and asking more questions. I had to tell them to forget it and moved on to the chapter about the nervous system—which should have included a section on the damage that can be done by repressing sexual urges in 16-year-old boys.

The ironic thing about this whole experience was that when we went to play basketball games at other schools, the janitor would come along to help me coach the team. And a female teacher would accompany us to help chaperone the kids. But then during the game, the two of them would disappear. They were sneaking away to do their own private biology course.

I, meanwhile, was ready to get away from all this hypocrisy.

Chapter 12

...And Straight Back to Paris

BACK IN MY BELOVED PAREE IN 1965, I DECIDED THAT I would study sociology. Not at the university, though—in night-clubs. And from now on, I decided, I'd be majoring in women.

I told a French guy about this new intellectual pursuit of mine and he said we should go to Le Bal de Sainte Geneviève. It was, he said, a huge old dance hall right near the Sorbonne, and on Saturday nights there was a dance that was frequented mostly by lesbians.

The next Saturday night at 10pm, I went along with this guy and was astounded at what I saw. A massive crowd of women, accompanied by even more women. The guy I was with was nearly the only male around. Though he looked a lot less butch than some of the girls.

A big band was playing all the old French standards from past eras: waltzes, foxtrots, rumbas, tangos, sambas, two steps. I gaped at a whole dance floor full of women-only couples. A hundred times more of them than the sparse crowd I'd seen at the Elle et Lui.

I nervously danced with a few women but without any chemistry or real flirtation. Then at midnight, an announcer said: "Mesdames, Messieurs, s'il vous plaît, sit down. Now we are going to put on a special show for you."

We all sat down while two professional dancers came on the floor—a man wearing a beret, red scarf, white shirt, black pants and a bolero jacket and a woman in a short red-and-black skirt with a white top. They started dancing a beautiful French tango. It was magnificent.

And then, little by little, they began having an argument in dance form, and he started acting a little violent towards her (still in dance form), until suddenly he was hurling her to the floor, pulling her hair, and dragging her around by the skirt. He picked her up, swung her around on his shoulder, threw her down again. She was pleading with him in dance mime, clutching his legs and begging for mercy, but he just carried on, getting even more carried away, strutting like a bull as he threw her from one side of the dance floor to the other, almost into the crowd.

Today we would label it domestic violence but back then in France it was called the *"Danse Apache."* Apparently, it had been very popular in the 1920s and was now recreated every Saturday night in this dance hall.

At the end of the dance, the man softened, he made seductive moves, and clutched the girl apologetically to his chest. The couple made up, and soon they were kissing passionately, to wild applause from the excited crowd. I thought, "Some women forgive their men much too easily," but I had to admit, it was an incredibly sexy show.

In the heady atmosphere after this display, my gentleman friend turned to me, grinning.

"Go and ask another woman to dance. Now is the best time. Everyone is excited." In French, the word *"excité"* has very sexual overtones.

Shyly, I looked around the room and I picked one out, a really cute woman I'd had my eye on for a while. I went and asked her to dance.

She said "oui" and we took to the floor for what the French call "un slow." It is what its name suggests, and it's the excuse to get in close and intimate.

After a couple of very enjoyable dances, we had a drink and chatted, and set up a rendezvous for the next day at the Parc Monceau, a chic garden in the west of the city.

And this time, unlike the German girl from Elle et Lui, she didn't blow me off. She came along to the park that afternoon, and we sat down on one of the benches, and chatted some more. Nothing very profound, just about who we were, but all the time we were smiling at each other as though we were doing a kind of verbal French "slow." After about twenty minutes she said, very matter-of-fact, "Why don't we go to my apartment? It's very close by."

I of course said "oui" and accompanied her a few streets away. We started kissing while we were still in the elevator and got straight down to business as soon as we were inside the front door. I didn't leave until the next morning.

But this wasn't love, it was sociology, so I said a polite, mildly affectionate, "au revoir," got in the elevator and didn't feel guilty about never getting in touch with her again. I was keen to delve even deeper into my new favorite subject.

* * *

I ASKED AROUND ABOUT THE names of other lesbian hangouts, and a couple nights later, I went along to one in Pigalle. This time I was alone, in a pretty sleazy neighborhood, and scared out of my wits.

It was a small club—a few women were dancing, others were just sitting and drinking, and they all seemed to know each other. I sat on my own for a couple of hours, getting bored as I listened to the Edith Piaf songs on the jukebox. Piaf had just died, and "Je Ne Regrette Rien" seemed to be the theme song of all the girls in this club. They would sing along every time it came on. But that just made me feel even more left out—an inexperienced American amongst all these knowing Parisians—and I thought that my experiment had failed, or maybe I just wasn't a good student of lesbian life.

I decided to leave, to catch the last *métro* at 1 am. On my way out, I went to the ladies' room, and while I was washing my hands, in came a young woman. She was cute, in a very boyish way, with short blonde hair and what looked like a man's suit. She smiled at me, and I gave her what must have been a slightly nervous smile back.

"Bonjour, mademoiselle," she said, very politely. "Ca va?"

"Oui, merci," I said, still washing my hands.

She smiled again and said, "Voulez-vous danser?" Did I want to dance?

I was surprised by this sudden pick-up in the washroom, and I'd been determined to leave, but I said "Oui."

"OK," she said, "can you wait for me? I have to...." and she nodded towards the cubicle, and we laughed. This girl really knew how to make me feel at ease.

We went back out into the dance area, and did a few French waltzes, face to face, old-style, and she told me her name was Michèle. She asked about my accent.

"Tu es Américaine?"

"Oui," I confessed. "Do you speak English?"

"Non." She told me she didn't speak a word of English, not even a song or film title. She had heard of "El-veess Press-lay" and "Ze Beet-ullss" and "Maree-leen" (she didn't add the "Monroe"), but that was all. Except "Gee-eff-ka".

"Who?" I asked (in French, of course).

"Gee-eff-ka."

Jeff somebody, I thought. A boxer maybe?

"Le président," she said. I realized she meant "JFK". That's what the French all called Kennedy. But that was all the English she knew, she said, except "whisky."

We laughed again. In a way, I felt relieved. If she knew nothing about America, she wouldn't have any prejudices. She would just accept me for who I was.

She asked me if I'd come to the club alone.

"Oui," I admitted. "Didn't you?"

"No, I came along with somebody else." Maybe I looked disappointed because she added, "it was just a friend." Interesting that she should let me know, I thought. "She's gone home now," Michèle added. "And I must go soon. I have to work very early in the morning."

"What do you do?" I asked.

"Contrôleuse," she said. I didn't know what it was, but it sounded very managerial.

"Contrôleuse?" I asked.

"Yes, on the buses. I check the tickets. I start at six in the morning."

"Oh, that doesn't leave much room for a nightlife."

"I'm not working on Saturday. Why don't we meet up on Friday night?"

I agreed, we gave each other a chaste goodnight, and she was gone.

I COULDN'T WAIT TO SEE her again. I hardly paid any attention to what I was singing to Monsieur Derenne, and I got completely stuck inside Jacques Lecoq's glass box. And the following Friday, right on time at 8 pm, I was sitting expectantly in a different club in Pigalle. It was hopping, very crowded, with everyone dancing and talking except me. But Michèle was not there. By 8:15 she still hadn't turned up. This wasn't too serious. Parisians are usually about 15 minutes late. They like to show you how busy they are.

I waited and waited, ordering two or three nervous drinks while I watched the door. Soon it was 8:30, 8:40, and I began to believe she would never show up.

Then, suddenly she came rushing in and gave me a huge smile when she saw me sitting at the bar.

"Excuse-moi," she apologized. "It sounds stupid, but my bus was late. We got caught up behind a garbage truck. We were half an hour late returning to the garage."

I was so glad to see her and she was so good at mimicking the driver trying to squeeze his bus past the garbage truck, that I forgave her instantly.

We danced and danced, and talked and talked, and I was having a wonderful time.

"Excuse-moi," she said again. "But I have to replace a colleague tomorrow morning. I have to go."

"Oh." I thought maybe it was an excuse. I'd noticed that I was a lot more serious than Michèle. She chatted, joked, laughed all the time. I was much more serious and I thought my amateurish French must have made me sound pretty stupid at times. Maybe she was bored already.

"It's very annoying," she said, kissing me on the lips. "I would have liked to continue our evening together."

"Really?" I felt a rush of relief.

"Really. Let's have lunch together on Sunday. I'm sure I won't be working then."

I said I'd love to, and she arranged to meet me on a *métro* platform.

"On the platform?" We were meant to meet up amongst a bunch of Sunday travelers? How unromantic could you get? But being new to Paris, I didn't realize that this is how many people meet up.

"Yes, Ménilmontant, line two, at noon."

It was a station I'd never even heard of, right up at the poor northern end of Paris, near Père Lachaise cemetery, but I said OK.

* * *

So that Sunday I took the subway way out to Ménilmontant, and sure enough, there was Michèle on the platform, at noon on the dot. We kissed—on the cheeks, of course, in public. Woman could not kiss openly back then. Then we took the train a few stops to Nation, the large square where there were several big Parisian brasseries full of people enjoying a Sunday lunch. Families, couples, all of them in a relaxed mood. It felt wonderful to belong to this typically Parisian scene.

Michèle and I chatted easily—she told me all about her job, squeezing through the crowds of commuters to sell or check tickets, stomping on the toes of the men who pinched her backside. I told her about my lessons, and mimed having a scalding hot coffee cup, and peeping over an invisible wall.

Then, as we finished our coffees, she popped the question.

"Would you like to come back to my apartment?"

"Oui," I said, without hesitation.

All the way there, she made me laugh. In the *métro* station, she ran to the top of an escalator, then began clambering back down the up escalator towards me. I'd never been with anyone who played around like this. Not since childhood, anyway. She was invigorating, exciting, alive.

We got off at Ménilmontant and walked to some modern-looking high-rise blocks. They looked poor, not at all classy like the Parisian apartments I'd visited so far.

Michèle's apartment was very spacious and there was nobody else there. Michèle said it was her mother's place but her mother was in the hospital because a truck had hit her and broken her hip.

"I'm sorry," I said.

"She's doing fine," Michèle said. "And now we have the place to ourselves."

We went straight into the bedroom, where there was a huge bed.

"Is this your mother's?" I asked.

"Yes, just let me check she's not in there." Michèle pretended to look under the covers, below the bed. I was still laughing as she pulled me down onto the blankets and began to undress me.

All I can say about the next few hours is that Michèle really knew how to punch my ticket. With her, my experimenting went way deeper than sociology. This was really in-depth research. It was mind-blowing. She did things to me and showed me what to do with her, things I had never imagined. After my swingers' party, this was my second awakening.

Eventually, when the afternoon ended, I returned to the Cité Universitaire in a fog. We had already made a date for our next rendezvous, and I trudged through the next couple of days like a zombie.

Then one morning, I went to join her on her bus as she took the tickets. She played up the scene for me, bantering with the passengers, and pretending that I didn't have a ticket and that she was going to call the police.

"This Américaine thinks she doesn't have to pay!" she told the other travelers. "But I bet she's rich. Have you got lots of dollars, mademoiselle?"

Her humor was infectious.

"Oh, please don't call the police," I begged her. "I'll do anything!"

"Leave her to me," a man said.

"Oh no, I'm taking care of her myself," Michèle told him.

It was much more fun than my acting classes, that was for sure.

I STARTED TAKING HER BUS regularly. That's how I got to know the different neighborhoods of Paris that were far away from my usual hunting grounds at the Cité U, St. Michel and Opéra. I was getting a thorough education in *everything* Parisian.

Michèle and I began seeing each other at least once a week. We would go on trips to the country for a day, and once we even went to the opera. We saw *La Bohème*, and Michèle told me it was the first time she'd been anywhere that fancy. It was certainly the only time I ever saw her in a dress with full ladylike make-up.

She preferred the world of night clubs and Pigalle. She took me to a burlesque club and we sat there whispering about the strippers, comparing their bodies, joking about which one we would like to have join us in bed. Afterwards she introduced me to one of the dancers, who was a "friend" (I didn't ask for more details). The stripper told me that she was a lesbian, too, and when she was taking her clothes off for the men, she would always imagine she was telling them, "here's one body you will never touch." It certainly explained the haughty look on her face as she stripped—which, ironically, drove the male spectators wild. It made me think about what went through performers' minds when they were on stage. I used this idea when I went back to mime school. I really imagined I would see the things I was miming, and I began to think, "come on, audience, can you *really* not see this?" It helped me a lot, and Lecoq even stopped bellowing at me, and began telling me I was getting good. I didn't dare tell him it was thanks to a trick I'd learned from a stripper.

SO MICHÈLE AND I GOT along great, laughed a lot together, and made fantastic love. I finally found out that she was half Jewish, because her mother had had an affair with a Jewish guy. That sealed the deal! Michèle was my belle.

She was a fascinating character. After a couple of visits to her mother's apartment, she told me it was in what New Yorkers would call the projects. It was subsidized social housing. These days it is a bit of a druggies' hangout but back then it was just poor and maybe a little shabby. Michèle told me that at first, she'd been afraid that an American like me would be snobbish about it but I told her I didn't care where she lived. What we did behind her closed doors meant more to me than anything else.

A few months after our first meeting, Michèle went up in the world. She passed the test to become a bus driver. In fact, she became only the second female bus driver Paris had ever had. I guessed this was one of the reasons she was so boyish. You had to be one of the guys to get ahead in that macho world. I wasn't complaining, though. She could dominate me all she wanted. A bus wasn't the only thing she knew how to steer in the right direction.

Chapter 13

A New Stage in My Life

I WENT BACK TO THE ELLE ET LUI CLUB, BUT THIS TIME NOT TO try and pick anyone up. This time I wanted to talk to the singer there, Maria. I wanted to go on stage.

Encouraged by my singing lessons, emboldened by the mime classes and talking to the Pigalle stripper, I thought I was ready to perform to a Parisian audience. I had also become infected with some of Michèle's daring. I told Maria that I was an American *chanteuse*, and for some reason she believed me. She'd never heard me sing, but said she'd try me out with one number, and if the crowd liked me, I could come back for more.

I'll never forget that night in the dressing room. I was a bundle of nerves as I watched the chorus girls at their dressing tables. I'd never seen more stunning women in my life. Their hair, their nails, their make-up, their jewelry, their long, smooth legs, they were all to die for. They were so much classier than the girls on the street of Pigalle, though in a glitzy, trashy kind of way.

Then one of them stood up directly in front of me and adjusted herself ... And I saw that this chorus girl had something very big in her panties. This "femme" was "un homme"! And much more feminine than me!

I was so innocent; I'd never realized that all these chorus girls were transvestites. Not that we called them that. I didn't know that word. Nobody did back then. We just called them "women with small hips." Or "women who got arrested if they went outside the club looking like that." These guys, or girls, were all selling themselves on the Champs-Elysées after the show.

I knew that singing in this club was my big chance, so I had got dolled up in my most glamorous dress (my only glamorous dress), lathered on the mascara and lipstick, and made my hair as bouffant as possible, which wasn't much.

I picked a song that couldn't go wrong. A song that was a huge hit in America. It was the theme tune to a brand-new Broadway musical. Everyone was singing it.

So, when Maria came to tell me I was next, I was more than ready. I was dying to go on and show everyone what I could do.

"Merde," Maria said as I walked towards the stage. Which of course meant "shit". Not very polite, I thought.

"Do you think so?" I asked her.

"It means good luck," she said. "It's what we say in France to everyone who's about to perform."

"Oh, merci."

"No, you're not supposed to answer."

"Sorry."

"Merde."

I was about to open my mouth but she shook her head and pushed me out on to the stage.

The audience applauded kindly as I went to sit at the piano, took a deep breath, and then starting giving it all I'd got: "Hello Dolly, well hello Dolly ..."

But they were all staring blankly at me as if I was playing out of tune or singing the wrong words.

No matter, I told myself, this was a massive hit, they were going to love it. So, I ploughed on, singing even louder.

"You're looking swell, Dolly...."

But they weren't looking swell at all. They were looking at the floor or the ceiling, or ordering drinks. They didn't give a damn whether Dolly was swell, or unwell, or even dead.

Merde! Or rather, not merde. I stopped in the middle of the song. By now an American audience would have been clapping and singing along, but these Parisians were still silent. They seemed to be waiting for me to get off stage so the real entertainment could start up again.

Well, that's tough, I thought. A Boston gal doesn't give up that easily. I hammered and shrieked my way to the end of the song, and then walked off to silence. No applause, nothing.

I went straight to the dressing room to get my coat. I couldn't get out of there fast enough.

But then Maria came backstage. She asked me what I was doing. Leaving, I said.

"But chérie, there is a second show!"

"A second show?" I asked her. "You want me to sing again?"

"Yes, chérie. But this time, sing a different fucking song! A French song!"

"OK," I told her, "you want me to be French? I'll be as French as they get. I'll be Piaf herself."

So later that night, I sat at the piano and gave the Parisians what they wanted: "La Vie en Rose." And even with my American accent (no American can pronounce "rose" like Piaf did, scraping her tonsils, making it sound like "hose" spoken while suffering from acute bronchitis), the audience loved me. They sang along, they swayed, they clapped, and they cheered when I'd finished as if I'd just brought Piaf back from the dead.

And by the way, since then I've sung "La Vie en Rose" more times than Edith Piaf ever did. Younger audiences these days know the song from the film *A Star Is Born*, where it's performed beautifully by Lady Gaga. But I'm sure Gaga must have seen my version of the song. In the movie, she performs it in a transvestite club, like I did back in 1964. And she sings it lying down, just like an 86-year-old woman. Yes, Lady Gaga is stealing all my moves.

Anyway, that night at the Elle et Lui, I learned yet another important lesson in life—if you sing to a French crowd in French, they'll love you. It doesn't matter what you sing as long as it's in French. For example, that Serge Gainsbourg song, "Je t'aime moi non plus", what the hell does that mean? "I love you, neither do I?" It's bullshit.

In the song, Gainsbourg sings, "je vais et je viens, entre tes reins"—"I come and I go between your kidneys." What is he, a surgeon? But who cares—it's French, so the French love it.

From then on, I was a regular at the Elle et Lui, bringing Piaf back from the dead every weekend. Or making her spin in her grave, maybe. I gave them "Milord" and "Je ne Regrette Rien", the whole catalogue. And they loved it.

I ALSO GOT SOME JOBS outside Paris. An agent saw me performing and offered me a gig in Tel Aviv. I would get a hotel room and full board he said, and a great salary, and would be going out there with a French *chanteuse*. OK, I thought, why not? I can study some of her moves.

Luckily for me, I didn't try to study *all* of them.

She was about my age, very friendly but taller and more beautiful—just how you would imagine a French cabaret singer to be. When we arrived at the Hotel Sheraton in Tel Aviv, we were given rooms in the hotel and we started working right away. I performed in a cocktail lounge that was part of the huge dining room, and I had to sing for about three hours a night. She sang with a band in the nightclub at 11 pm but only for a half hour and for more money than I was getting. (Where was the French *égalité*?)

I thought the hotel was getting a good deal out of me, but after a week they told me I had to move out of my room. They were sending me to stay in a bedroom in an apartment with no air conditioning. It was hot as hell. The French singer though, got to keep her suite in the hotel. It was totally unfair.

Then I found out what was happening. Every night, the hotel would make sure the *chanteuse* got a date after her show with one of the guests. And she would spend the night with him—all part of the five-star service. In fact, she was a singing hooker. I was shocked. Not so much about the fact that she was sleeping with lots of guys—hell, I would have been into that. No, it was because she told me that most of her clients were Americans, married men, mainly Jewish jewelry dealers, with families back home. She would show me all the rings and bracelets she received from the guys the morning after. My image of the nice Jewish family man was destroyed forever!

I did get to date a few Israeli guys but I soon figured out that they were all after a green card, to get them out of Israel. One Iranian Jew explained to me that there was a pecking order in Israel amongst all the different nationalities who had moved there. On the top rung were the Americans, French and British, then the Germans, the Poles, and at the bottom were the Jews from the Middle East, Iran, Iraq, and at the very bottom, the people from Yemen. This pecking order determined who you would socialize with, what college would let you in, and what kind of job you could get. He told me that the Yemenites swept the streets. This was a big awakening about my view of Israel. I could see why he wanted to come to America, but I told him sorry, I wasn't going to take him home.

There was one guy I nearly did take back with me but he was Greek. On my way back to Paris, I stopped off on the island of Hydra. It was wild there. I used to sing in the cafés and nightclubs till one or two in the morning. There, in one of the cafés, I met a young guy from Athens who was an artist, and he painted me nude every night. The sex was great, but one night when we were jumping around, I fell over and hurt myself. I was in agony, and could hardly breathe, so I rushed back to America, where X-rays showed that I'd broken a rib. Talk about Greek wrestling.

What I regretted most wasn't the pain, it was the paintings. In my haste, I had left Greece without any of the nude pictures. Today, they're probably on some old guy's wall in Athens.

But all this travelling and singing had given me a great money-making idea....

Chapter 14

"Try Not to Be So Jewish"

BY NOW THE SIXTIES WERE GETTING SERIOUSLY SWINGING FOR ME. I was making the most of it, performing in a transvestite club, going to swingers' parties and hooking up (and laying down) with my regular girlfriend, Michèle.

Maybe my parents sensed that I was having just a bit too much fun. They didn't know anything about my love life, of course, except that I wasn't remarried. But one day they wrote and told me that my niece (my brother's daughter) was getting married, and said I had to come back to Boston for the family celebration.

Well, I didn't want to leave Michèle and she definitely didn't want me to go.

"It wouldn't be for long," I promised her, though I wasn't sure that was true. I wrote back home telling Mom that it was a long way to come just for a niece's wedding. Michèle was very grateful and showed me in some extraordinary ways.

Just after that, a cousin who was in the liquor business, and often travelled to France, came to see me. He took me to a fancy restaurant and laid on the family pressure.

"Everyone expects you to be there. It will be a big family occasion. Your brother will be so disappointed. Your mother is in a state of nervous exhaustion worrying about you. She can't understand why you don't want to get married again yourself."

Well, he didn't say it all like that. He interspersed the arguments between glasses of wine and brandy. Getting mildly drunk on French booze was part of his job.

"Have you got a boyfriend in Paris?" my cousin asked.

"No," I said truthfully.

"Don't you want to find a new husband?"

"Not really."

"I'm sure you could do better than the first one."

He was right about that, though he had no idea that I was already doing much better with a woman.

"Just come back for the wedding and see how you feel," my cousin said. "Your Dad will wire the money for the ticket. Or I can advance it to you now."

I think that despite myself, I was feeling guilty about being a lesbian. And my cousin was a very skillful ambassador for the family.

"OK," I told him. "I'll come back home, but just for the wedding."

I broke the news to Michèle the following day, and she was really upset. She begged me not to get on the ship.

"It won't be for long," I promised her again.

And again, she didn't believe me. The next night she turned up at my room in the Cité Universitaire. Both her forearms were bandaged. She told me she had cut both her wrists, then chickened out and gone to the hospital to get the wounds treated.

I was horrified, and in a cruel way, her desperation made me even more determined to go home. It would be wrong, I thought, to give in to that kind of blackmail. I had to go back to Boston, attend the wedding, then return to Paris to prove to Michèle that I cared for her.

I got on a ship at Le Havre and cried for the entire five-day trip across the Atlantic.

To soften the blow of leaving Paris, on my first weekend back, I met up with one of my oldest friends.

This was Johanna. I'd met her at girl scout camp in Vermont when I was 16 and she was 14. One Sunday at camp, we walked together to the Federation Church, where we were going to sing in the choir. It was about a mile away, and we got chatting. We found out that we were both Jewish, and thought it was funny that we were going to sing in the choir of this Protestant church. It turned out that Johanna was a New Yorker, born in Czechoslovakia, who had escaped to America to flee the Nazis. It was fascinating to hear her tell stories, like how when she was four years old, she had had to wander around the streets of Paris while they were waiting for their visa for America.

I was always a goodie-goodie girl, but after church that day, where we'd had lunch, we were cleaning up the tables, and started throwing wash cloths at each other. I had never been so wild, and we laughed so much. A couple of weeks later, when she went home, I was sure I'd found a friend for life. Afterwards, though, we'd gradually lost touch, and I hadn't heard from her in at least ten years.

Anyway, that first weekend back in Boston, I went to a play in Cambridge, and when I came home to my parents' house, I was told that Johanna had called. I was astonished. I called her back, and she was living just a mile away, with her husband and two kids. We chatted as if we'd never been apart, and we became best friends again.

Of course, I couldn't tell her and her husband everything I'd been doing in Paris, but maybe I told them just a little too much. Because one day the husband called me and said he needed to talk.

"Sure," I said, "go ahead."

"Not on the phone. Can you come over?"

"Of course. When?"

"Now."

I thought this was a little bit strange, but I drove over, and when I got there, Johanna wasn't home.

"She's taken the kids to her Mom's place," he said.

I asked what he needed to talk about and he looked embarrassed.

"You were living in Paris," he said.

"Yes."

"I bet you saw some things."

"You mean, like the Eiffel Tower? Sure."

"No, I mean, I bet it was wild, right?"

"During the summer sales? Yes, really wild."

I guessed what he was referring to but I didn't really want to go down that road.

"No, I mean... you must be *experienced*." He wasn't talking about golf.

"A little," I said, feeling a stab of guilt about Michèle.

"Johanna is not experienced at all," he said.

"But you've got two kids. Isn't it your fault if she's not experienced?"

"It's not exactly about experience. More about being *adventurous*."

"You want her to take you to the Amazon jungle or what?"

"Well, a little jungle savagery would be a good thing," he said, and looked at me in a way that suggested I might be the wild thing he was looking for.

When he kissed me, for some reason, I didn't resist. Maybe I was missing the sex I'd had with Michèle. Maybe my guilt about making her sad made me feel a responsibility to console someone else, like Johanna's husband for example.

We ended up in bed. And compared to my ex-husband Seymore, this guy wasn't bad. Not as delicate with his fingers or lips as Michèle but attentive and passionate. So we started meeting up regularly for sex, and even though I was betraying my friend, I have to admit I enjoyed it. The fact that Johanna might walk in and catch us only added to the excitement of the adultery. Once a *Parisienne*, always a *Parisienne*.

AFTERWARDS, I WENT HOME AND wrote a long letter to Michèle, promising her that I'd be back soon, and saying how much I missed her. And I meant it all. But the wedding came and went, and I kept putting off my return trip to Paris. Michèle sent a couple of chatty letters, then they started to turn bitter and recriminating, and I got a little scared of her. And meanwhile I was meeting up with Johanna's husband for regular trips to the jungle.

I was in a real mess.

ADDING TO MY CONFUSION WAS my uncle, the founder of the Berklee School of Music in Boston. Maybe he was under pressure from my parents to convince me to stay in America, I don't know, but in the spring of 1966, he started advising me to move to New York, where there were plenty of performing jobs. That was what I wanted, wasn't it? To perform, like I'd been doing in Paris? Well, here was my chance and New York had far more openings than Paris. I was on home territory. I could end up on Broadway!

Naturally, I was tempted. With my parents' help, I rented a tiny studio apartment in the middle of Greenwich Village. It was at the start of the hippie time. I didn't know a soul and would walk around the Village feeling shocked by all the young girls in T-shirts but with no bra. (Remember, I'm from Boston).

This was when lots of people started smoking marijuana. I was very innocent about that. One day I met a nice guy somewhere in the Village and he invited me to a party that night in his apartment. I got there at around eight and almost nobody was there. I listened to some music, had a few drinks, chatted to the host of the party, and then finally, a couple of hours later, crowds of people started wandering in, and they all sat down on the floor and started smoking. I wasn't sure what was going on but everybody was really quiet, and stopped talking.

They kept offering me to share their cigarettes and it finally occurred to me that it was a pot party, and everyone was getting strung out. I'd been to much wilder parties, of course, where dozens of people took off their clothes and started making love in front of everyone but then they'd been drinking champagne and cognac. But these were drugs, illegal drugs! I left as fast as I could!

A few days later, a nice person who lived in the building next to me said they were having a party that evening, and asked me to come. When I arrived, nobody was smoking—instead they were all arguing about the Vietnam War. They were trying to figure out what they could do to stop it—write letters, demonstrate, hand out leaflets, etc. I had never seen people in Boston so passionate about politics and I was astonished. I felt uncomfortable and left that party early too.

I just didn't fit in. Swinging, stripping and sexual exploration were fine, but pot and Vietnam? Count me out.

I wrote to Michèle telling her that I missed her and Paris. That our times together had felt so free and natural compared to this weird stuff that was going on in New York where I felt so out of place.

Of course, she wrote back saying "come home to Paris!", and I was touched. But I just couldn't go. Not yet, anyway.

I started spending a lot of time in a café around the corner from my apartment called Sutters. It was a French place with croissants and espressos—everything that reminded me of my favorite city. Well, nearly everything.

And this was where I hit on my brilliant money-making scheme: I was going to be a professional *Parisienne*.

Yes, I decided, I would *become* Edith Piaf. She had died and left a huge gap in the market. I, like a true American entrepreneur, would exploit that gap. After all, I could sing in French which almost no Americans could do, and I knew all the songs. I'd even performed them in Paris. Added to this, I knew that if I was going to get work as a performer in New York, I needed a unique selling point. The city was overflowing with singers. But they didn't have an Edith Piaf.

MAYBE I SHOULD CONFESS THAT I didn't get the idea in a flash of genius. It came to me slowly. Well, to be brutally honest, it was forced upon me.

Sure, like my uncle had told me, there was more work for performers in New York, but of course there was also a lot more competition.

For months after I arrived in New York, I put on slit skirts, sequins and low-cut tops (which I could never have done if I'd stayed with my parents in Boston) and accepted every job I was offered.

One of the first engagements I got was playing piano at a hotel Christmas party.

A guitarist called JT called me up. He was a graduate from the Berklee School of Music (why else do you think he called me?). JT asked if I could play rock 'n' roll and I said of course, though I didn't know a thing about it. I'd completely missed out on the rock 'n' roll and pop revolution. Musically, I was still back in the age of Judy Garland, Doris Day and Edith Piaf, of course. With me it was showtunes and ballads, nothing rocky at all.

But I had sworn I would accept anything, so I went along to the gig at a boring, business-type hotel in Brooklyn. It was a party for a bunch of people from the same office, who were of all different ages, and all different stages of drunkenness, even right at the start of the evening. They just wanted to party, so it didn't really matter what we played.

JT told me we'd be playing a load of standards, like "Roll Over Beethoven". Now of course I knew about Beethoven but I never knew he rolled over. And now I was actually sitting at a piano, I thought I'd better confess.

"I don't know any rock 'n' roll," I told him.

To my surprise, he just shrugged.

"No problem. It's all the same song, basically. I'll yell out the chords to the first one, and you'll see. Just follow me."

So that's what he did. He screamed out the chords as we did the songs, the singer and the drunken audience screamed out the words, while I jammed along, and we were a huge success.

At the end of the evening, as JT handed over my share of the night's money—a generous $25—he asked me if I wanted to do more shows.

"Of course," I told him.

"Not just rock 'n' roll," he said. "Do you know any Irish music?"

"None at all, apart from 'Danny Boy'," I confessed. I guessed he wouldn't care, and he didn't.

"I'll give you some sheet music, and the rest you can busk, like you did tonight."

JT was Irish Catholic, so our backgrounds were wildly different, but we shared a love of music and performance, and from then on, he booked me for all sorts of Irish events in Brooklyn. So in fact, before becoming French, I became Irish.

JT was married at the time but we dated a little. By which I mean, we slept together at my apartment between rehearsing Irish folk songs. It was just a bit of fun for both of us. I was still writing regularly to Michèle, planning to go and visit her as soon as I could.

Then, weirdly, JT started to get less Irish Catholic. He began to lose his identity. And one day he told me he was joining a Hawaiian band. About as far from Dublin as you could get.

AFTER JT STOPPED BEING IRISH, I needed to look for work, but I ran into a major obstacle: my nose.

Well, let's get this straight (as a good nose should be). People always say that the entertainment business is monopolized by Jews, which is racist bullshit of course, but in this case, my Jewish manager started telling me that I was too Jewish.

To be fair, my uncle had warned me. As a young man, he'd been in a trio and played all over New England. He told me that when they drove up to some hotel in the White Mountains, there would often be a sign in front, saying "No Dogs or Jews Allowed." But I thought, that was before the War, things must have changed by now. Well, apparently not that much.

My manager, who, at the risk of repeating myself, was Jewish, explained one day in his office:

"Before the bookers even meet you, there's the problem of your name. Diana Shulman isn't a performer, she's a

Brooklyn housewife. You have to change it if you want to be in show business."

"You mean, call myself something like Candy Shulman?" I asked. "Or Ritzy Shulman?"

"No!" he said, so mad that he even took his cigarette out of his mouth. "Even in the Catskills, which is Borscht Belt Central, they want their crooners to be Gentiles. You got to lose the Shulman!"

I couldn't believe this Jewish manager telling me to stop sounding Jewish. But then, I reasoned, show business is all about pretending to be someone else. Wasn't john Wayne's real name Mary?

"How about my mother's maiden name, Lunn?" I asked.

"Sounds Chinese," he told me. "You want to sound French."

"How about Edith, then?" I suggested.

"Edith? Doesn't sound French at all. Sounds like a Connecticut grandma."

"But Edith Piaf was French!"

"Well, she doesn't sound like it to me. What else have you got?"

I had a think and all I could come up with was a French-sounding version of my own first name, Danielle.

"Great!" the manager said. "Danielle, nothing else. Very French. Leave the rest to me, Danielle."

And he started to get me jobs in clubs and hotels as a French *chanteuse*. Nothing too well paid, but it was work, and I was getting good at acting the *Parisienne*. I wrote and told Michèle that she wouldn't recognize me when I came back to see her.

Which turned out to be truer than I'd planned, because a short while after I changed my name, I hit another problem.

My manager sent me to see a booking agent, a woman in Brooklyn who only booked Jewish events. She had told him that she had a great regular gig on offer, and was really keen to fill it with one of her acts. It was to entertain once a week at a Jewish Beach Club in Brooklyn for the whole summer. My manager told her that Danielle the French *chanteuse* would fit the bill perfectly.

So, I went to see this woman in an old office building near Brighton Beach, the kind of place where you find private detectives in the movies. She looked just like my mother but smoked ten times more, and swore, which my mother never did.

"Shit, you're Danielle?" she said as soon as I walked in the door.

"Oui," I told her, trying to keep in character.

"You don't look French. You look Jewish."

"I am, so what?" I asked, too shocked to stay French.

"All right, shit," she said, looking me up and down. "We'll send the club your resume, without a photo. By the time they sign the contract, it'll be too late to pull out."

So flattering. But I really needed the work and the money, so I agreed.

And while I waited to see if I'd got the job, I received yet another punch on the nose, almost literally.

Another Jewish agent, a very important guy in the business, came straight out and told my manager that he refused to get me any work unless I had a nose job. Mine wasn't a bad nose, but he told me manager it was "ethnic". By now

I was getting the message loud and clear—my name was wrong, my face was wrong, I came from the wrong side of the American religious divide.

I called my mother to tell her the awful things that were happening to me in New York. But her reaction wasn't what I'd expected.

"Finally!" she said.

"What do you mean, *finally*?" I asked.

"I've been telling your father for years that you ought to get a nose job."

"What?" I couldn't believe this.

"Yes, it will boost your career, and your chances of picking up another husband will be *greatly* improved. Do it!"

Ah, Jewish mothers.

So Mom sold her blue-chip stocks to buy me a blue-chip nose. And after that, I could pass myself off as a WASP, even a French WASP. I'd go to a club or hotel, sing "La Vie en Rose" and the owners would say "oh merci, Danielle," and try to talk French with me. They swallowed the whole charade.

My French image was helped by a happy accident. I got a one-off job playing and singing for a young and middle-aged Jewish crowd at an oceanside hotel not far outside Boston. The gig was on a Saturday night, so I turned up early and spent the afternoon at the beach, swimming and sunning myself.

When I went on stage at 9pm, I found out to my horror that my voice had almost disappeared. I guess salt water and sunstroke were not ideal before a show. I was croaking and almost whispering as I sang, and thought the crowd would hate me. But they loved it. They seemed to think I sounded like a genuine French *chanteuse* who'd smoked too many Gauloises and drank too much absinthe. Encouraged by their applause, I even started to talk some of the lyrics, and just be sexily French.

After a few songs, I went out into the audience singing "C'est Si Bon", the classic French ditty made famous by Yves Montand, and began to smooch suavely between the tables. All of a sudden, one 50-something woman started beckoning me over. As soon as I got within reach, she grabbed me, and sat me on her lap with her arms wrapped around me. I was surprised, but true to the rules of performing, I kept singing and smiling until the song was finished. Again, the crowd loved it. They bought right into the idea that for a French woman, anything goes.

Clearly, my new identity as Danielle was going to take me to new, exciting places. If I could get both men and women excited about me, *anything* was possible.

My *Parisienne* persona worked so well that sometimes, actual French people would ask me if I really was French.

"Bien sûr," I would tell them.

"But you have an American accent," they would say (in French of course).

So I'd tell them, "Oui, that's because I was born in Paris but brought to the USA at a very young age."

They usually believed me.

SOMETIMES, I COURTED TROUBLE FOR myself. I started getting bookings at huge senior women's luncheons around the New York area. Sometimes there would be a French theme, but occasionally it was an Irish afternoon. So of course, I would go along, do Irish songs and claim to be from Kilkenny. Then at one of these Irish parties, some women came over after my first set and said, "Hey, weren't you the singer at that French luncheon? Are you French or Irish?" I guessed that they were Irish, so I told them I was only pretending to be French, and that my family was really from Kilkenny. They laughed and congratulated me on fooling everyone. Well, they were right about that.

OF COURSE, THEN CAME THE cold shower. Absurdly, a German restaurant turned me down for a job because they said "Danielle" was too French for them. After being too Jewish for the Jews, I was too French for a place that wanted a "French" singer?

I was horrified. Next, people would be telling me that I sounded too Gaelic to be Irish. Or that I played piano too well to play in bars. Was there no way of being accepted? All I wanted to do was entertain, and yet everyone kept questioning whether I had the right to entertain them, all because of who I was or who I wasn't. It was amazing to me. This was the 1960s, supposedly the time of freedom, be yourself, free love, equal rights, and yet segregation was as bad as it had been when I was at college, or before the war when my uncle used to play. Of course, I wasn't suffering as badly as Martin Luther King and the civil rights activists, but I knew how they felt to be excluded.

I started thinking seriously about going back to Paris, where no one had ever stopped me doing anything because of who I was—on the contrary, they had encouraged me to break every boundary there was. But when I mentioned the idea to my parents, they told me, no way. I had to stay in the States. They were still helping me with my rent, so I couldn't argue.

ONE DAY, IN A FIT of depression I went to pour my heart out to a friend. She listened patiently and then told me to "seize the moment". A new nose deserved a new name, she said.

So we opened up the dictionary that I'd received from David Gorfinkle, and, to get inspiration, looked up my real first name, Diana. It said that she was the Greek goddess of hunting and the countryside. We also read that Diana was meant to be a virgin goddess, but it was too late to worry about that.

"Goddess of hunting? That's perfect," my friend said. "Go back to calling yourself Diana. But you need a second name. Maybe something to do with the countryside."

We brainstormed for a while, and finally hit upon Forest. (I decided that Diana Rabbit or Diana Plow wouldn't have been so good.)

Diana Forest sounded OK, but it was still a bit banal. So, we morphed plain old Diana into exotic (but not ethnic) D'yan, pronounced "Di-aaan". And D'yan Forest it has been ever since.

THAT WAS MY PROFESSIONAL IMAGE more or less taken care of, but my private life seriously needed livening up. I'd finished my affair with my best friend Johanna's husband (they'd left

America for Brazil, not because of me, I hoped) and seen my Irish guitarist lover turn into a Hawaiian, so now there was a bit of a blank.

I couldn't go back to France (not yet, anyway), because of my parents' continued opposition to the idea, so I decided to relive some of the excitement of Paris by going to a swingers' party in New York. The people there were all very educated and good looking, well-spoken and well dressed. After some polite talking, the clothes came off, the mattresses were laid on the floor, and everybody started mixing. But for some reason, I found it boring. Maybe the Parisians had spoiled me. Maybe I was nostalgic for Michèle. I don't know.

I was thinking about leaving when a very handsome guy came over beside me and said: "Hello, who are you?"

He was intelligent, charming, and he asked for my phone number. We went out on a date, and met for a drink before dinner. We were chatting and laughing about the party we'd been to, and everything was going fine, but when I told him I was a cocktail pianist, playing five nights a week, he was turned right off. The atmosphere suddenly turned as cold as the ice in my whisky.

"What's wrong?" I asked.

He shook his head and shrugged.

"I want a full-time lover. Someone to meet up with whenever I want. Not just the odd evening when you happen to be free. I can't date a bar singer."

And he finished his drink and left. I was so astonished at this brutally frank outburst that I hardly reacted at all.

Here was someone else rejecting me for what I was. People had rejected my religion, my name, my nose, at least two of my fictitious nationalities, and now they were rejecting my job—no, more than that, my vocation, my dream.

I'd had enough of America. Financially, I was more stable. My grandfather had bought me a small apartment on West 10th Street, so I didn't need help with rent. I'd saved up some money from working so regularly. So just before Christmas 1967, I told my parents I'd been offered a gig playing in Paris, and left.

Chapter 15

The Call of the Wild

MICHÈLE AND I HAD BEEN WRITING TO EACH OTHER, AND WE'D both come to realize that even if we played around with other people, and even if I had male lovers, there was something deep between us that lived on. Our letters had lightened up. No more recriminations, just chat, sharing news and stories. When I saw her again after more than a year, it was as if I'd never been away. Except for my new nose of course.

We took up where we left off, dancing in Pigalle, going to dinner in glitzy places that she'd never dare go to alone, and spending plenty of time in bed—mainly at my hotel. It was heaven for me. To be accepted again, to feel free to be who I wanted, to be away from disapproval and criticism. It was everything Paris has ever meant to me.

Sometimes, while Michèle was at work, I'd ride on her bus to be near her and people-watch Parisians. At other times, I'd wander off alone in search of new experiences.

* * *

ONE OF THESE HAPPENED IN Pigalle. It was on a winter's afternoon. I walked past a brightly-lit doorway marked "Spectacle"—erotic show. I'd been to a couple of strip clubs with Michèle, but they were fairly tame places, where women just took their clothes off while clients drank and talked. From the photos outside, this place looked more hardcore. There were naked couples, apparently in the full act of making love. It was outright pornographic.

Wondering whether I should go in there alone, I went to a café across the street and had an espresso. From the café, I stared at the Spectacle Érotique sign until eventually I decided, yes, I have to try it.

At the entrance there was a man behind a very tall desk. He was listening to classical music. He smiled and said, "Bonjour, madame, you know this is not just a strip-tease?"

"No?" I asked innocently.

"No, it is a sex show. Are you OK with that?"

"Oh, oui!"

I paid the money, (a discount for Americans, he said) and then walked down a dimly lit, curving stairway with a smoothly polished rail. I emerged into what seemed to be a medieval cellar, decorated like a sultan's harem. Velvet cushions on a comfortable bed, golden lamps all around, beaded curtains hanging from the ceiling, and mysterious nooks and crannies, all dimly lit.

Piano music was playing, and I peered into the darkness and took my seat among a dozen or so men. This wasn't a bar, it was a theater, with rows of seats facing the stage, where two naked women were just getting up from the floor (it was the end of their show). They vanished upstairs, and the men and I all sat there, hands in our laps, staring silently at the empty stage before the music began again. The atmosphere was heavy and sweaty.

Down the stairs came a long-legged, high-heeled woman in a dress that was slit up to her waist. Her entrance was accompanied by a very sexy French song, crooned by a sultry *chanteuse*.

The newly arrived *femme fatale* moved all over the room, pouting alluringly at all the men, who were spellbound. She began dancing, using every muscle and curve in her body to full erotic effect. This went on for a few minutes, but I felt we were all impatient for something more than dancing. At last, she slowly started taking off one glove, then the other, and threw them into the audience.

Then came off the shoulder straps, one at a time, and she sat on the lap of a guy in the second row, and wiggled a bit. It was not quite a lap dance, it was more subtle than that, and she let him put his hand on her back for a second. Then she jumped up, went back on stage and started to take off the rest of her dress, pulling it down, down, down—until it slipped to the floor. I'd seen stripteases before but this was more controlled, more nuanced, and I was captivated.

Now she was down to her garter belt, stockings, black panties, and the skimpiest bra I'd ever seen. She had a fantastic figure, too. Dressed (or undressed) like this, she began dancing and flirting languorously with the guys. She even came to my side of the room, where I was sitting hunched inside my coat, scared that someone from Boston would come in and recognize me. She sidled past me, to get to the guy on the other end of the row, and I was tempted to reach out and stroke her perfect skin.

Then she went down to the stage again, and started taking everything off until she was wearing nothing but her high heels.

I was tempted to run away, but I was totally spellbound too, especially when, to the rhythm of the music, she started to pleasure herself. The temperature in the room went through the ceiling.

But then she came to some kind of fake climax, the music stopped, she stood up, collected her clothes which were strewn around the stage, and said in a very un-sexy voice, "Merci, I am Bernadette." And then she vanished up the stairs.

From fake climax to anti-climax.

WE ALL SAT IN SILENCE again for about two minutes, and then loud British rock music blared out, and down the stairs ran a beautiful young woman who was dressed as an English school-girl in the appropriate uniform. She cavorted about the stage, pulled off various items of clothing, then lay down on the floor, and got on with the real business at hand, if you get my drift.

At which point I got bored. It was so fake. I'd seen the real thing at swingers' parties, where the stripteases were all faster and more amateurish, but the sex was real.

What was really interesting to me in this club was the men's reaction.

Down at the front, there were several really old guys. During one of the acts, one old man kept leaning further and further towards the stage, and then got on the stage, staring intently at the action. The stripper stopped touching herself and sent him back to his seat like a naughty school-boy. Maybe he was just short-sighted. Or maybe those old guys had never even looked at their wives' nether regions. They were making up for lost years.

When I had first walked in, all the guys had turned to stare at me, then looked back at the stage. But one of them kept turning around and eyeing me. I didn't know if he wanted me to come and sit on him, or whether I was cramping his style. I just sat there hunched up in my coat, and didn't react. After a while, he got up and left, so I guess he just didn't like being watched by a woman as he ogled women. Or maybe I looked too much like his wife.

One of my favorite acts down in that basement was a belly dancer. She had all the bells and spangles, and was fantastically nimble with her gyrations and her finger bells. I'd seen plenty of belly dancers in the Catskills. I'd even been on the same bill. Even in the Orthodox Jewish Bungalow Colonies, a singer like me was often just an opening act before the star belly dancer. The guys there would be undressing her with their eyes as she danced. But down in this Paris basement, there was no need. This belly dancer removed everything, until she was dancing with nothing but a chain around her waist. Oh, I thought, if only those guys in yarmulkes could see this!

Though they would probably have been less interested in the German dominatrix who came on stage with her whip and handcuffs. Too many bad associations.

AFTER AN HOUR AND A half came the final act. The true climax.

There was a total blackout, and then the lights came up to reveal a woman dressed in white, frozen like a doll in a fixed position. Another woman danced around her, trying to get the doll to move. She pulled at one arm, then the other, and slowly the doll started to come to life. She started to teach it how to move well, how to dance, and then how to kiss. It was all very mysterious and exciting, and when the two of them began making love to each other, for once it looked real.

And the girl who had been doing the awakening must have sensed my excitement, because she came up to my seat and straddled me as I sat there. She gyrated against me and even placed my hands on her breasts. She let her hair flow down into my face and I drank in the sensations. I was totally lost.

Then of course, the music stopped, she got up, and the girls went upstairs. It was, after all, just an act. And that's what you've got to remember in these strip joints. The girls on the guys' laps, or on stage taking their clothes off, or even while they're "masturbating", are just thinking, "five more minutes and then I can go smoke a cigarette", or "damn, I forgot to empty the washing machine."

But it was fun, and very enlightening, and I decided to go back again. I'd finally understood why men went to these places.

Weirdly, just as I got back to my hotel room, Mom called.

"So how was it?" she asked me.

"How was what?"

"Was it really all velvet and gold?"

I thought, my God, had someone from Boston seen me in the strip club? Was it that guy who'd stared at me and suddenly left? He'd gone out and called my parents and told them he'd just seen Diana Shulman in a sex joint?

"Was *what* velvet and gold?" I asked Mom, playing innocent.

"Versailles of course. You said you were going to the Château of Versailles."

"Oh, yes, Ma. Versailles was beautiful. All velvet and gold. Marie-Antoinette wasn't there, though. They terminated her lease."

"What?"

Thank God for that, I thought. It was a shock to think that my parents could ever get an inkling of the kind of things I'd been getting up to. Mom wanted me to marry, but she probably thought I was still necking with boyfriends and waiting for a proposal. It would kill her to know I was making love with people—men and women—whose names I didn't even ask, or getting sat on by Parisian strippers and bus drivers.

I realized that I'd come a long, long way from life in Newton, Boston. But this who I was now, and I was happy with the way I was. I wanted to go on living it to the full, even if I could only find true freedom a long way from home, in France.

* * *

AT THIS TIME, THE QUESTION of my identity also pushed me in another direction.

It's an ancient cliché that behind the mask, all clowns are sad. Well, with my background, I had good reasons to possess a deeply serious side. And I had never been able to answer the question as to why the European side of my family got massacred. Or what kind of people would do such a thing to them. Or even tacitly let it happen.

The mild forms of discrimination that I'd been suffering—even from people of my own background, made me want to delve much deeper into my historical identity.

During one of my first stays in France, early in the 1960s, I met two lovely German sisters from Hanover, Germany. Margot and her younger sister were living in Paris as au pair girls in order to learn French. They were around my age and we became fast friends. They were the first German people I had gotten to know.

They went back to Germany, and said I had to come and visit them, so I wrote and asked if the invitation still stood.

They said yes, so I set off on the long train ride across Europe that so many people of similar origin to my own had taken twenty-odd years before, in much more horrific circumstances. Trundling across Germany, looking out at the hills and woods, I couldn't help imagining all the people, including kids of my age, who had made the trip in window-less carriages in the early 1940s.

When I got to Hanover, I was fascinated. I had never been to a German city before, and I kept looking at every older German person, wondering what they had been doing 20 years earlier, and even how many Jews they had killed.

However, I found Hanover itself slightly boring, except for Margot, her sister, and their friends. And as far as I could tell, there was nothing really interesting to do in the area. It wasn't until I got back to New York that I read, totally by accident, that Hanover was only about thirty miles from Bergen-Belsen, where Anne Frank had died.

I was astounded that Margot had never told me that this notorious death camp was just down the road. The only conversation that we all had about the war was when Margot's sister said that Hitler really wasn't all that bad because he had built a lot of highways, and had done a good job of building up Germany's economy. I, of course, didn't argue with them because I was their guest.

Now, a couple of years later, and back in Paris, I called her up and said that I would love to come back to Hanover, and this time go to Bergen-Belsen. There was a short silence on the line, and then she said she didn't have a car. But then she seemed to relent.

"OK," she said, "somehow we will get there."

"Yes," I said, "maybe we can use one of those famous highways."

But when I arrived in Hanover a few days later, Margot wasn't at the station. I looked all over for her, and finally a visitors' bureau took pity on me, and called her up. Margot told them that she'd been waiting on the platform, and when she didn't see me get off the train, she had gone home. (She probably hoped I'd changed my mind.)

I took a taxi to her place, and the next day, a friend of Margot's with a car took us up to Belsen. I was terribly nervous going there. I imagined a vast torture chamber, piles of bones, lines of unmarked graves.

But in the end, it was a bit of an anti-climax. All I could see was a huge field, with nothing on it except a few little stone memorials erected by groups from Israel. Nothing left—except a museum at the very far end of the area. And when we went into the museum, everything was described in German, and it's not one of my languages, so I had a hard time figuring it out. And Margot was no help. I saw a photo of some very healthy women. Margot said that they were prisoners. I didn't believe her, and I was right—it turned out they were the female concentration camp guards.

Then Margot said she wanted to visit her aunt and uncle nearby. We walked literally five minutes away from the camp, to a cute little farm, where we found the aunt and uncle, an ordinary-looking old German farming couple. Margot told me that this was where her parents had sent her during the war, and where she grew up. I was speechless. It was all I could do to stop myself from asking them if they knew what was going on a block away. But I didn't have the guts to say anything—I was a guest and thought I should keep my mouth shut. In any case I didn't speak any German. To this very day I regret not asking.

But then I knew the answer already—*of course* they knew what was happening at the death camp down the road. How could they not know? How could they not try to stop what was going on there? Or at least express some regret to me now, or simply their sorrow at the crime that had been committed against all of humanity just a five-minute stroll away from their cozy home? This was denial like I'd never known it before.

To a certain extent, I understood denial. I'd seen people at Middlebury hiding their identity to protect themselves against prejudice. I'd hidden my own identity to get jobs. But no one was threatening these old Germans with discrimination or unemployment. And they were the ones who'd been complicit in a crime, unlike me.

It didn't answer my question about why the concentration camps had existed, but it did suggest *how*. It just takes enough people to close their eyes and ignore the problem.

Leaving Belsen (unlike so many of its previous visitors whose voyage through life had ended there), I decided that this was going to be a lifelong mission. I was going to visit other camps, and build up a full picture of the horrors that had been committed. I was going to do the opposite of denial.

Chapter 16

New York, Loves and Farewells

I WENT BACK TO NEW YORK, DETERMINED TO KEEP MY PROMISE to Michèle that I'd return soon. And this time I knew it was all up to me, and that no one could stop me anymore.

This didn't mean I took a vow of chastity, of course. I was enjoying my freedom too much.

Right on cue, some old loves popped back into view.

My friend Johanna and her husband had come back from Brazil, and he called me up and we started meeting again to fool around. I felt really guilty, but I liked the guy, and more than ever after my visit to Belsen, I was determined to live life to the full.

I also thought Johanna would never find out. Then one day she phoned me and told me she knew what was going on.

I didn't know what to say, but she hadn't called to yell at me.

"I don't blame you," she said. "I caught him messing around while we were in Brazil and he told me, 'I was having an affair with your best friend, too.' Nice guy, right?"

"I'm so sorry, Johanna." I meant sorry for her, for what she'd been through.

"It's not your fault. He is a serial skirt-chaser, and you got chased. I guessed he'd started seeing you again, so I thought I'd call you and warn you. He's been playing around with his secretary, and I'm going to divorce him."

He'd been living life to the full, just like I had.

"Well, I don't think I'll want to see him again," I told Johanna.

"Me neither," she said, and we laughed together, and promised to stay friends. Which, by the way, we still are, seventy years after we first got together, throwing wash cloths around in church. These days we're a bit better behaved.

MY OLD FRIEND BEN SAILED back over my horizon, too. This was the guy who didn't want to go out with a cabaret singer. Well, now it seemed he'd changed his mind. He invited me out on a date, took me back to his apartment and showed me exactly how interested he was in this particular cabaret singer.

We started seeing each other regularly, and sort of became girlfriend and boyfriend. We had a lot in common. We both played tennis, we loved skiing, and we loved swinging. He even asked me to marry him. Non-stop for a whole year. But I always refused.

Two reasons: number one, after three consecutive days together, he always started to bore me. He just wasn't exciting. That was probably why he kept swinging, even when we were together. He had to be with people for short periods of time, otherwise they'd get tired of him too. Plus, of course, I was still very committed to my long relationship with Michèle. My attraction to Ben wasn't half as strong as my connection with her. In truth, he was little more than a tennis and sex partner.

Number two, he was tight with money and I hate that. I'm naturally generous. If I have cash, I invite people to lunch or dinner. He was the opposite.

At one time or another, we travelled all over Europe together, but believe it or not, he never bought me a single cup of coffee. Not even an espresso. We'd get the check and he'd start to complain and say, "How much is that in dollars?" and I'd say, "Forget it, I'll pay."

The most glaring example of his tightness was at a ski hotel in Courchevel, France. We were stranded in a blizzard for two days. Skiing was impossible so after walking around in the snowy streets we would return to the hotel in the afternoons and everyone would drink at the bar to pass the time. Since I spoke French, we socialized with all the French people there, and they started to buy us unusual French drinks, like those spirits with a pear or a peach marinating in the bottle. We were having a ball. But it was one-way generosity from the French.

One of the women asked me: "How come your *ami* never buys us any drinks in return?" I told her how tight he was, and bought rounds for everyone myself.

I think Ben's tightness was just one part of his egomania. He only ever thought of himself. One time we were in Chamonix, in the French Alps. I had broken a rib in New York a week earlier, and was told by the orthopedic surgeon that I could go skiing but had to avoid steep slopes, in case I fell over. I explained this to Ben, of course. After we settled into the cheapest hotel he could find, he said, "There's a great slope I'll take you up, not too steep, we'll go this afternoon."

We went up, up, up, up on a cable car in the middle of a blizzard, and then proceeded to ski down a slope that was not only as steep as a cliff, it was also covered with five feet of fresh, treacherous snow. And smothered in fog.

Skiing was almost impossible and I kept falling down on my broken rib. My screaming threatened to cause an avalanche at any moment.

Slowly, turn by turn, fall by fall, I made it to the bottom, but it took hours.

When we got back to the hotel, Ben was very apologetic... and then he tried to have sex with me. I told him to forget it and didn't talk to him for two days.

A FUNNY THING HAPPENED ON that trip. For some reason, torturing myself on the slopes hadn't put me off skiing for life, so I wanted to buy new ski boots. We went to the sports store and I spent an hour trying on boots, and when we came out into this beautiful little street in a quaint medieval French mountain town, there were police everywhere. I asked what had happened, and I was told that the bank next door had been robbed while I was trying on my ski boots. The robbers had escaped down into the valley before the police knew what was happening. At the end of the week, I read in the French newspaper that the cops had caught up with the robbers in

Marseille, on the south coast of France. They'd cornered one thief, totally naked, in the shower in his apartment, and shot him dead. I've always wondered what a naked bank robber could have said to the cops to make them shoot him.

AFTER OUR SKI TRIPS, BEN and I would always end up in Paris and do the sights together. Naturally, I would spend time with Michèle, and to his credit, he never minded. He was happy enough going to strip clubs and swingers' parties while I had fun with my long-term girlfriend.

I was grateful to him for this openness. And for another nice thing. One day, despite my vociferous refusals, he made me climb to the top of Notre Dame. I'd never done it before. We puffed all the way up there, and stood right next to the huge ugly gargoyles that are so famous. I was able to look out over the whole city, from the very center of town—a much more intimate view than from the top of the Eiffel Tower, which I could now see pointing up at the sky in the distance.

But I found that, instead of looking out across the roof-tops, my eyes were drawn down to the streets below. I was fascinated by the people walking there, and the buses, one of which a certain girl might be driving. I felt at one with the Parisians more than anyone else on the planet. It's a feeling I've never lost.

JT THE GUITARIST ALSO MADE an appearance. I'd lost all contact with him, but then one night, a taxi stopped beside me in Chinatown, and JT got out, along with a Filipino girl.

Apparently, he'd divorced his first wife, joined a Hawaiian band and married one of the other musicians.

After that chance meeting, we stayed in touch, and he started to get even less Irish Catholic. He got hair transplants, ostensibly to look younger, but began growing his hair longer and longer, until one day he showed up in my apartment with high boots and a flamboyant shirt, and I said, "JT, are you becoming gay?" I had nothing against that of course, but he denied it: "Oh no, I just have to look this way for a show in New Jersey."

Then one afternoon a few years later, I turned on the TV and saw a story about a transvestite who had been using the ladies' room at Loehmanns. They said he was a guitarist from Brooklyn, and at the end of the segment, I saw it was JT.

I called him up, and someone answered with a sweet, high voice.

I said, "JT is this you?"

He said, "Yes, I took hormone shots and had my Adam's apple removed. This is the new me."

The strange thing was that he'd stayed with his wife, except now everyone thought they were sisters.

So for a few years, through the 1970s, I had this crazy, bohemian life that was fulfilling in a chaotic way. In New York, I was performing regularly, making good money, getting more and more authentic as Edith Piaf's re-incarnation. I had a regular boyfriend, Ben, and a regular (though less frequent) girlfriend, Michèle, whom I visited for at least two months every year. She would also come over and visit me and we would take trips to places like Disneyland and Niagara Falls. Our relationship was as fresh as ever. It didn't go anywhere, but it didn't fade either. Both of us were happy with this state of affairs. We had fun when we were together, and when we were apart we wrote letters, sent each other cassettes on which we recorded our thoughts and stories, while also living full lives on our own sides of the Atlantic. I also dated other people if they attracted me and made me laugh, or sing, or just feel comfortable.

I was now D'yan Forest, doing my own thing, and at last New Yorkers seemed to accept me for who I was. Either that, or I didn't care what they thought anymore.

THEN CAME THE FIRST SIGNS that my life might be changing.

Returning to New York after one of my Paris jaunts, I got a call from a policeman.

He asked me, "Do you know Ben Hershon?"

"Yes, is something wrong?"

"He's been found dead in his apartment."

Being the guilty type, I immediately said, "I've just arrived back from Paris," in case Ben had been murdered and I was a suspect.

But the cop told me Ben had probably been dead for three weeks or so. His mail had been piling up, so his janitor finally went into the apartment and found him in bed.

The police called me because I was the only one in all those weeks who had left their phone number on his answering machine. Before leaving for France, I had called him to ask him out to dinner. He didn't get back to me right away, so I called again the next day and kiddingly said on his answering machine, "Hey Ben, don't you know my number anymore?" and left my number. And now I found out why he never returned the call. He must have been dead already.

Even Mary, Ben's most regular girlfriend at the time (he had quite a few), hadn't contacted him. But when I told her he was dead, she was grief-stricken and said we had to give him a funeral. So we found an apartment on the Upper East Side where all his friends could meet on a Sunday afternoon.

When I arrived, I saw a lot of people that I knew. They were all men and women from the swinging scene that I had been in with Ben. I hadn't seen them for years, but evidently Ben had continued getting together with them.

We all gave a little speech during our makeshift service. This was before I had started my comedy career, so it was unusual for me to speak in front of a lot of people, but I ad-libbed about my adventures with Ben, and I got lots of laughs.

On the way home after the get-together, I was in the taxi with Mary and she told me she had had a date with Ben to play tennis one Saturday, just before I left for Paris. She said that she had gone to his apartment building early in the morning, but he never answered the buzzer when the doorman rang him up.

I asked her, "Why didn't you ask the doorman to let you in and find out if anything was wrong?"

She said, "Oh I thought he might be in Las Vegas with a girlfriend or somebody else. He was always going away."

I was shocked that she hadn't gone up to try and see Ben. Maybe he could have been saved. We will never know. But I will never forget that taxi ride.

Everything about Ben's death saddened me. His nephew in Washington, who was his closest relative, got all his money but never came to retrieve the body. Finally, Ben was buried in a Veterans' Cemetery in Long Island, as he had been in the US Marines during the Korean War. I'm pretty sure I'm the only one who has ever visited his grave.

THE OTHER SIGN THAT MY life was about to change came from Boston.

It was September 1981, and I was about to fly off to Paris for a couple weeks. My brother Herbie called me, which wasn't a frequent occurrence.

"You've got to come to Boston right away," he told me.

"Why? What's wrong?" I was terrified it would be bad news about my parents.

"Nothing's wrong. You have to drive Mom and Dad to a wedding in Marblehead tomorrow." This was an hour north of Boston.

"But today is Friday, and I'm leaving for Paris on Monday."

"I don't have enough space in my car. You have to take them."

"So, you're invited to this wedding?"

"Yes."

"But you can't take Mom and Dad?"

"No."

Well it all sounded crazy to me, but I said OK, and left New York very early the next morning (a four-hour ride) so I could pick them up. I arrived fine, and we made it to the wedding ceremony right on time. When the reception started, we were all milling around, and I noticed my mother and father mixing in with everyone, chatting, having a good time. I saw my mother had a white drink in her hand and asked her what it was. She said it was a sombrero, and contained Kahlua and milk. I had never heard of it, so I got one and it was delicious. We all had a great time at the wedding, and I drove my parents back to Boston and slept over.

Next morning, the Sunday, I had to leave as I was flying out to Paris from New York on the Monday. My mother was asleep when I was getting ready to leave, but woke up, and yelled from her bedroom, "Goodbye and have a great time in France!" She still had no idea what kind of things I did when I was there.

As soon as I got back to New York, my brother called me. I assumed he was going to say thanks for taking our parents to the wedding, and enjoy your trip. But no, it wasn't that.

"Next week, Mom is going into a nursing home."

I couldn't believe he was telling me now. He had probably been scared of my reaction. We'd talked about this with her and Dad, and she agreed that it might be better if she had regular care because she'd been having more of her unstable spells. But I'd visited half a dozen homes, and none of them were suitable. All the residents were drugged up and just sitting in the common rooms staring at the television and not saying a word. This was not my mother.

"Mom is OK with it," Herbie said.

It sounded suspicious to me, so I called her.

"Are you really sure, Ma?" I asked her. "Have you visited the place?"

"Oh yes, don't worry, Diana. I'm going there next week. You have a good time in Paris."

What could I do?

I flew to Paris, and spent the afternoon in bed with Michèle. But my heart wasn't in it. For some reason I kept imagining that Mom was in the room with us. Not exactly conducive to wild sex.

So that night I went out alone to a night club, but I was jet-lagged, and so was everyone in Paris, it seemed, because no one talked to me or asked me to dance.

I was staying with my friend Mado, and when I arrived home at 1 am, she was still up, waiting for me, and she told me my father had called her at midnight. I had to phone home.

Terrified, I did so, and my father answered the phone right away.

"Diana, your mother passed away yesterday evening."

"Oh God, how?"

He explained. It was Rosh Hashanah and Mom had wanted to go and buy some flowers for the holiday. She asked the caretaker of my parents' building (they were now living in an apartment) to come with her. Together, they walked a few blocks to the store, but while they were in there choosing flowers, there was an armed robbery. Mom fainted with shock. She was taken to hospital and died there. She was 82.

My first thought was, how spooky! Was that why I'd imagined my mother in the bedroom with me and Michèle? Mom's spirit had flown the Atlantic to say goodbye? Well, if so, she must have had quite a shock when she found me.

"The funeral is in three days," my father told me.

I booked a ticket for the next day. Michèle consoled me, but she seemed sadder that I wouldn't be staying in Paris the whole two weeks than she was about my mother. And talking to her, I realized why I hadn't enjoyed my time in bed with her the previous day. I still had guilty feelings about enjoying this secret life in Paris, and they had come to the surface while I was with Michèle. And from now on, I thought, my mother would be watching every time I did *anything*. It was a harrowing thought. (That fear stayed with me for two whole years, before I decided that she had risen to a new world and was no longer observing me—which was just as well given the kind of stuff I was about to get into.)

I flew home to Boston and my father picked me up at Logan airport and took me to view my mother. I went alone into the room where she was lying in the coffin, and she looked so real, so alive, that I said to her,

"Wake up Ma, wake up!" I kept trying to talk to her, bending over the coffin, trying to attract her attention so she would come out of this sleep, and behind me I overheard her sister, my Aunt Sally, saying bad things—my mother had been crazy, she'd been cruel. It was so thoughtless. The two sisters hadn't talked to each other or seen each other for 20 years, but that was no reason to be so mean. It hurt me to think that families can be so divided when they should be united in grief and solidarity.

I talked to Mom for quite a while.

"It was because you didn't want to go into a home, wasn't it, Ma? You preferred to die." She didn't answer, of course. But she didn't contradict me, either. I was sure that some part of her had rebelled against the idea of ending up in one of those common rooms, surrounded by half-dead residents.

The funeral next day was horribly painful. I cried the whole time. The next day I went back to New York to fetch some clothes so that I could stay in Boston for a while to take care of my father. I had to cook for him. He didn't even know how to boil an egg.

My father's sister, Aunt Minnie, said that I should come back to Boston and live with my father. I really thought it over and was on the verge of giving up my apartment in New York when I called my shrink. I told her what had happened, and about my conversation with Aunt Minnie.

"Don't do it!" my shrink told me. "You have to live your own life. That's always been your biggest challenge, living the way you want to, doing your own thing. Now you have to do it. You can go back and visit your father as often as you like, but you have to have your own life."

Well, that was what I paid her for.

Like I said, I was devastated by my mother's death for the next two years. I would scream in agony and cry my heart out. I guess we all live in a world where our parents will never die. I was so devastated that I didn't travel abroad for two years. Michèle was really mad at me, accused me of neglecting her, but I couldn't do it. There were limits to living my own life.

I used to visit Dad a lot, and once when I was staying with him in Boston, my brother came over and I heard him and my father talking in the other room about "ripping up the will." I went in there and demanded:

"What are you talking about? Excluding me from Mom's will?"

The two of them looked embarrassed. My father was a nice man, but he was of the era where the women weren't meant to be concerned with legal details, and where only the male children counted. So, my brother Herb was the sole executor of both my parents' wills, and I had absolutely no say in anything. But at least I managed to stop my brother and Dad from ripping up my mother's will, so I got a small gift from her. All the rest of her cash and belongings went to the men, of course.

My relatives in Riga, Latvia, in the 1920s. By 1945, almost all of them had been murdered by the Nazis.

My first and last time deep-sea fishing. In Miami with my niece, nephew and my brother Herbie. I have the souvenir stuffed on my wall (the fish, that is).

Dyan Forest

My New York Swing Sixties look, after the nose job.

In the 1960s, Pigalle was the place to go to get yourself photographed with naked shoulders.

Trying to get work as D'yan Lunn after my Jewish agent told me to drop my "too Jewish" name.

A memorable photo: in the 1970s I showed my cleavage on stage for the first time.

D'yan Forest

I had to buy this hand-held keyboard to perform in clubs where they wanted me to walk around serenading the customers.

An agent's ad in the 1980s. I sang in nine languages, two or three of which I actually understood.

How many 85-year-old women take a trip into the wilds of Ethiopia?

Wannsee, near Berlin, outside the cute villa where the Nazis decided on their "final solution."

2019 Ladies Club Champion:
Karen Levinson
Runner –Up: Pat Kerrigan
Net Club Champion: D'yan Forest
Congratulations Ladies!!!!

Susan Morrissey had a HOLE IN ONE
on the 5th hole on August 5th
Lawrence Howard had a HOLE IN ONE
on the 8th hole on August 15th

When I was 85, I beat youngsters of only 60 years old to win this golf championship.

Rehearsing for my slot on the TV show *France Has Got Talent*. Why else would I wear an Eiffel Tower hat?

The poster for the show about my scandalous
adventures as a *Parisienne*.

Winter in Montmartre, Paris, suffering for a publicity shot. The
show ain't over till the old lady freezes.

Chapter 17

I Married a Nun

IT WAS IN 1983, ABOUT TWO YEARS AFTER MY MOTHER'S DEATH, that I met Nell the nun. She had just moved to Southampton, on Long Island, after divorcing her husband (yes, some nuns have husbands). And she'd brought along the five-year-old daughter she'd had after cheating on her husband with a friend (yes, some nuns have illegitimate children, too).

Maybe I need to give you some background.

I was interviewed for an article in one of the Hamptons' newspapers, and when it was published, the writer, a lesbian friend of mine who called herself Artemis, came over to my apartment in the Village with the newspaper, hot off the press, to show me. I was thrilled. It was the first article about me in the media. Before she came over, Artemis phoned ahead and asked if it was OK to bring a friend with her.

"Sure," I said, "who is it?"

"She just arrived from Puerto Rico."

"Great, a ray of tropical sunshine!"

"Well, she's not *from* Puerto Rico. She was just living there. She's from Long Island."

"Oh, OK." Not quite so exciting, after all.

"She used to be a nun."

"A nun?" Even less exciting. I guessed Artemis was dragging this friend around to liven her up a bit after all those years in a convent. "Bring her over, though. What's her name?"

"Nell."

"Nell? As in death knell? Great!"

It turned out, though, that I was wrong to be pessimistic. Nell was lively, lovely, a lot of fun, and cute. She was taller than me (which wasn't difficult), and good-looking in a boyish kind of way.

We all went out for lunch in the Village, and Nell gave me an edited version of her life story.

"I put on the cowl just after high school," she explained, while biting into a hunky grilled cheese sandwich and a mug of beer. This former nun clearly enjoyed the pleasures of life. "It was a Catholic school," she said, "and I'm pretty sure the principal got a bonus for every girl she turned into a novice. She convinced me to sign up by telling me the convent would put me through college for free—which they did, except as well as studying, I had to cook and clean all day for the 'qualified' nuns. They kept telling me, cleanliness is next to Godliness, but in my case, it was next to slavery."

We laughed at Nell's ironic take on nunnery, but this wasn't the worst of it.

"Every Saturday," she said, "they made us novices join in flagellation sessions."

"Flagellation?" I'd heard the word before, but only in Parisian sex clubs, outside the rooms where SM fans shut themselves away to experiment with the whips and chains and handcuffs.

"Yes. The nuns used to lock us novices all together in a room decorated with nothing except a crucifix and a painting of the Virgin Mary looking sorry for us. And we'd have to stand in a circle, and then we'd lift up our habits and whip our naked backs with a thin metal chain."

"Oh my God." Artemis and I were listening as if Nell was describing a cheap porno film.

"So there was this circle of bareback nuns, squirming and whipping ourselves, occasionally letting out a squeal of pain, but trying to keep quiet because we didn't want to give too much pleasure to the sadistic nuns who we guessed were listening outside the door."

"Wow." I could picture it so clearly, and was wondering whether it was erotic or just sick.

"No wonder I turned out kinky," Nell added, which was the clincher—erotic it definitely was. "I mean, here was this gang of sexually repressed teenage girls, half-naked, doing SM in front of each other. So of course, while I was at the convent, I fooled around with a few of the novices. And a couple of the priests, too. They used to come and hear our confessions. And I used to give them the whole lot, in technicolor detail. Believe me, after that, they wanted me to perform a whole lot more than a few Hail Mary's."

"Did you get thrown out of the convent?" I asked.

"No, the Mother Superior offered me missionary work in Puerto Rico. I didn't think I'd be any good converting other people to Christianity, but I accepted. Maybe I just misunderstood what they meant when they talked about giving me 'a missionary position'."

We had a great lunch in the Village and I decided I definitely wanted to see Nell again. I was going to be in an Off-Broadway play and I invited her to come along. It's always a good seduction technique to get someone to watch you on stage.

Then at the last minute, Nell called up to cancel. Her daughter, she said, had scarlet fever.

"Daughter?" The nun had kids?

She explained. While she was doing missionary work in Puerto Rico, teaching at a school, she'd also started taking scuba lessons.

"You got pregnant during a scuba lesson?"

"Not during. After." She explained: "I didn't usually wear my habit, and the scuba teacher liked the way I looked in a diving suit, so one New Year's Eve, he invited me to come and celebrate in his lighthouse—and I stayed the whole weekend. When I got back to the convent in San Juan on the Monday, I found a note on my bed ordering me home to Long Island to see the Mother Superior. Evidently the other nuns thought that scuba wasn't the only kind of diving I'd been doing. So, I went home, got thrown out of the order because apparently it was OK to whip semi-naked girls, but not to party with naked scuba teachers, and went right back to Puerto Rico."

"To live in the lighthouse?" I asked, feeling more excited about Nell with every confession. I understood those priests at the convent.

"Yes, and we got married, and I did all sorts of jobs—all-night bartender in a gay club, fast-food street vendor, placing buoys for the coast guard. Dead-end stuff. I wanted to have a baby, but my husband had had a vasectomy, so I used to wait until I was ovulating, then meet up with a married guy for sex."

"Oh my God." This was the kinkiest nun ever. She had been experimenting even more than me.

"Six months later, I got pregnant and had a baby girl, who I called Angela."

"Were you trying to convince your husband the baby had been conceived by the Angel Gabriel?" I asked. "What did he think?"

"Well, by this time he was turning into a drunk, so after five years, I moved back to my family in Southampton, and here I am. Sorry about not being able to see your show. When can we meet up?"

As soon as possible, was what I wanted to say, but I had to wait a few weeks until I was invited to a women-only party out in the Hamptons. Nell came along. It was a hot summer night, and after a few glasses of wine we all decided to go for a swim in the pool. None of us had swimsuits so we went skinny dipping. Nell invited me to sleep over at her place and we stayed there together for the next 25 years.

I LOVED HAVING A YOUNG daughter. I taught Angela to swim, I introduced her to golf, and I used to enjoy taking her to musicals on Broadway, which she adored. Nell was a great cook, and we often spent evenings at home when she would make us Puerto Rican food and we'd laugh and talk about everything and nothing, and I felt deeply content and complete. I loved being part of a family.

The only thing I didn't love was the rooster in the yard who would wake us up at 4 am every morning. And when Nell borrowed a gun and shot it, I thought that was true love.

She also had a parrot, an African gray, that she'd brought back from Puerto Rico. She loved it, and insisted on keeping it in a cage in our bedroom. It spoke three languages, which was very impressive, but it used to start talking them at seven every morning. Not so great. It also used to crack sunflower seeds all day, so I was constantly walking on a carpet of nutshells.

I complained to Nell, but it didn't do any good until one day the parrot disappeared. We looked for it everywhere—out in the woods, in the streets, around the whole neighborhood. We had just given up hope when Nell got a call from the new owners of the house she used to live in down by the beach.

They asked her, "Is your parrot missing? Because we have one in our chicken coop, hanging out with the hens."

We drove over there as fast as we could, and as soon as we arrived outside the house, Nell leapt out of the car and whistled. In a flash of grey feathers, suddenly the parrot was there on her arm.

Nell was relieved, but it made her think that maybe the parrot was unhappy in its cage. It wanted to be back near the beach. So we came to an agreement. She needed money to pay the rent, and I wanted to keep the parrot out of our bedroom. It was a deal: the parrot found a new home, and Nell's rent got paid. Call it blackmail, but just try sleeping in the same room as a parrot who squawks at you in Spanish as soon as the sun comes up.

And no, it wasn't me who took the parrot to that beach house.

Chapter 18

An Outsider Amongst the Outsiders

NELL AND I BOTH LOVED PLAYING GOLF. THE PROBLEM OUT ON Long Island was that there were always long waiting lines at the public courses, where the greens were usually crowded with duffers trying to hole that final putt after visiting every sand trap along the way. (Yes, I'm a golf snob.)

There were a few private courses in the Hamptons, but they never accepted Jews, Italians, Blacks, or Catholics. Naturally they didn't announce this to the world. It was just that, to join their club, you had to be recommended by somebody whose family came over on the Mayflower.

One day I was playing tennis with a friend, and I asked how come her boyfriend wasn't playing with us. She said he was playing golf at the club nearby, with her parents.

"But they're Jewish!" I said. "Do they let in Jews to that club?"

"Sure," she said. "It was founded 30 years ago by a bunch of people who couldn't join any of the other private clubs."

She explained to me that these outsiders had bought a large plot of land in the hilly forest, and then went around asking people for 5,000 dollars to buy a bond, become a member, and help pay for the building of the golf course. They got enough money for nine holes, built those, and then collected the funds for the second nine. I was dumbfounded.

When I got home, I told Nell, "I've found a private golf course that will accept both of us! A Jew and a Catholic!"

I assured her that this wasn't some idealistic golfer's version of the afterlife, and we drove straight out to the club.

As soon as we got there, Nell told me to turn around and leave.

"We'll never fit in," she said.

"Why not?"

"Look at those cars."

I saw what she meant. It was wall-to-wall Cadillacs.

"I don't want to be with these kinds of people," Nell said.

"You're not a nun anymore," I told her. "You can't expect everyone to take a vow of poverty."

"I don't want to take a vow of snobbery, either," she said.

"Let's go and inquire," I begged her. "Maybe Cadillacs are just what they use as golf carts."

We went in and talked to the secretary, who was very friendly, but told us that there was a long waiting list.

So many outsiders trying to get accepted as insiders, I thought. Too bad.

"But there is one way of improving your chances," the secretary told us.

"Buy a Cadillac?" Nell said.

I told her, gently, to shut up, and asked what that was.

"Buy a bond from someone who's leaving the club, or who died."

"I can arrange that," Nell said, but whispered it this time, fortunately.

"How much is a bond these days?" I asked.

"About twenty thousand."

I gulped. That was just to get in, before you started paying the fees.

"You have a friend who's a member?" the secretary asked.

"Yes." I told her about my tennis buddy's parents.

"Get them to invite you for a game." She really was being helpful. I loved this place already, even if beside me Nell was fuming with social resentment.

I played a round with my friends' parents and her boy-friend, and the course was perfect. With all the hills and trees, it reminded me of Maine, where I used to play with my parents.

I bit the bullet and cashed in some bonds to buy a golf bond from a family whose father had died. Then I called up the secretary and asked when I could become a member.

"It's not that simple," she said. "There's a waiting list of people with bonds."

"What?"

"You could buy another bond. That would convince the club that you're really serious. We have a member who's leaving soon. Do you want me to put you in touch?"

"Sure." I could almost hear the sound of my bank account creaking under the strain.

But I bought the second bond, and six months later, we were asked to come for an interview with the board members. It was less of an interview than a cozy chat that didn't feel at all cozy. I chatted with an Italian guy about my singing and piano career, and Nell talked with a Swiss American woman about our skiing in the Alps. It was all very tactical. If there'd been a Jewish board member, I'd have shown off my Yiddish.

Two days later, the secretary called me up.

"You're in!"

"Both of us?"

"Both of you."

"That's wonderful. It was worth spending all that money."

"Ah, well you haven't finished spending yet."

"What?"

She explained that we (or rather I) had to pay up another thirty-five thousand dollars apiece.

I couldn't believe it. Seventy thousand? Just to play golf.

"Well, there aren't many clubs in the Hamptons that have our open policy," the secretary said, politely reminding me of my outsider status. I knew she was right. I wouldn't even get an interview at the other places.

"But seventy thousand," I sighed.

"Yes, it's a lot," the secretary agreed. "Unfortunately for you, it's higher than usual because the club needs a new sprinkler system."

I was ready to pass out, but then I remembered the money that my Aunt Sally had left me. She passed away at the ripe old age of 104 and left me a generous inheritance. But should I really use it all to help pay for the golf club's sprinkler system?

What the hell, I thought, you only live once.

"OK, seventy thousand," I said.

The secretary said that would do nicely.

We were in! Hallelujah! That June we started playing golf on this wonderful course.

THE CLUB TOLD US WE could enter the Ladies' tournaments, which took place on Tuesdays. A little discriminatory, I thought. I have a decent handicap, so I can hold my own against most men on the golf course. But what the hell, we started going along on Tuesdays.

We dressed up as prettily as we could, but compared to the other members, we looked like country hicks. We quickly bought golf fashionable clothes so that we'd fit in.

However, we noticed that whenever we finished playing, most of the ladies were sitting at one table eating lunch, and there never seemed to be any room for us. It was the same every time.

I had a quiet word with the secretary who looked a little embarrassed, and said she couldn't imagine why anyone would not want to sit with a charming couple like us.

But I got the message. A charming *couple*. We were labelled gay. All the other ladies were staunchly heterosexual (in public, at least), and we didn't fit into their network. We had no husbands who could do anything for them or their husbands, businesswise or socially. And they didn't want to take the risk of getting invited to a lesbian barbecue, right?

I couldn't believe the irony of it. I'd found the one club in the Hamptons that didn't discriminate against me because I'm Jewish, a club founded by people who wanted to stop feeling like outsiders, and now they were making me feel like an outsider.

What could I do? Look around for a club founded by non-WASP gay people? But then they might discriminate against me because I'm bisexual. Or because I'm an entertainer. Or not as tall as them. Or because I like pizza. I realized then that I'll never fit in. I'm always going to be someone's outsider.

Still, at least I could play golf with Nell. Here was a gay lapsed-nun single mother who accepted me for who I was.

Or so I thought.

Chapter 19

The Route to My Roots

MY NEVER-ENDING FIGHT TO AVOID GETTING JUDGED FOR who my ancestors were made me even more determined to go to Europe and face the truth about what real hatred can do. Even while I was in the midst of my battles with the golf courses, I knew that there are more extreme ways of expressing prejudice than refusing membership of a club or not inviting people to lunch.

So, I dragged Nell across the Atlantic to my family's old country, Latvia. I needed to see Riga and the place where my relatives had been forced into hiding or just plain massacred.

This was the mid-80s, before the Iron Curtain came down. The curtain was rusting, but still in place, so Americans were viewed as rich cash cows to be milked of dollars, as well as potential enemies in a nuclear conflict. It was a very unsettling atmosphere.

We went via Saint Petersburg, which was still called Leningrad. It was a mixture of baroque splendor and Soviet grimness. All those magnificent palaces, and the fabulous art at the Hermitage, combined with waiters like prison guards and side streets that smelled of old cabbage.

Ordinary stores with almost nothing in them alongside dollar stores stocked with real coffee, candy and American booze.

Then we went to the real target of the trip—Riga. I wrote to my cousin Yetta but never got a reply. I figured she was probably dead by now. So I was in Riga as a tourist. Though not many tourists were there to see what I wanted to see.

Ignoring the Art Nouveau buildings and the old town, I went to the ghetto. Almost nothing remained of it, except some notice boards talking about Nazi oppression, and some photos of troops herding columns of people through the streets. I studied the photos but they were blurred, blown up, and I couldn't see faces.

Nell and I found a taxi driver who could understand English, and I told him I wanted to go out into the forest where the Jews had been killed. At first, he didn't understand. I guess most tourists don't ask that kind of question. I mimed a machine gun mowing people down, and, no doubt thanks to my training in Paris, he understood what I meant.

He drove us a frighteningly short distance out of town, only about three miles, into dense woodland. It was a beautiful summer's day, very hot sun, but the air in the woods was fresh and cool, and the only sound was bird song. We stopped in a clearing, and the driver said,

"Here, fascists kill."

I just hoped he didn't mean they were still at it.

Nell and I got out and walked along a narrow path into the trees until we found some square earth mounds that apparently marked the areas where the bodies were buried. They were grown over with grass and fresh flowers. It seemed impossible that such a peaceful place could have seen such horror forty years earlier.

There were grainy photos set up on the mounds, presumably of victims. I looked at the faces, some of whom were smiling. They must have been pre-war pictures. Amongst the innocent faces, I found children who looked just like me at that age. It sent a cold shiver down my spine to think that if my grandfather hadn't left when he did, my photo might be on that mound right now.

There was no real explanation of what went on there. Back then the massacre site wasn't set up as a true memorial. We tried to ask the taxi driver but his English wasn't up to much beyond "fascists," "kill" and "you pay me dollar?"

I would have liked to explore the forest and find the place where my cousin and a few other Riga Jews had managed to survive, but that was impossible. The driver didn't even understand the question. Which was predictable. After seeing the massacre site, it was impossible to believe that anyone could have survived.

Again, I had to wonder what the taxi driver's father and mother were doing while my relatives were being force-marched out into the forest. Maybe they were in the Soviet army resisting the Nazi invasion. Or maybe they were just watching the procession.

STRANGE AS IT MAY SEEM, the visit to Riga only whetted my appetite to find out more about concentration camps, and the people who knew about them.

Next on my list was Auschwitz, though it took me ten years to get there.

Again, I managed to convince Nell that we could take a vacation in the less glamorous parts of Europe, and we flew east. By now it was 1995, the Berlin Wall had been knocked down and sold in pieces to tourists, and Poland was free of Soviet rule.

Not that traveling was easy.

This was before Auschwitz became a major holocaust tourist destination. We arrived in Hungary, then flew to Warsaw where we paid a taxi driver $300 (an absolute fortune) to take us to Krakow. We had to take a taxi because we couldn't figure out the train schedule in Polish—ironic, a Jew who couldn't get to Auschwitz by train. What was worse, young kids kept trying to steal our suitcases.

The driver took us speeding through the countryside and Nell got scared. I said it was nothing to worry about because everybody in Europe drives like this. Then five minutes later, skidding around a curve, we almost bumped into a wagon, upside down by the side of the road, with the horses that had been pulling it lying dead. I guess I was wrong about not worrying.

The next day, our driver took us to Auschwitz, or Oswiecim as the town is called. Wow, what a difference from Bergen-Belsen. Belsen had been nothing but a big empty field. Here in Auschwitz, all the buildings and train tracks, the barracks and latrines, crematoria and watchtowers, the barbed-wire fences and the infamous "Arbeit Macht Frei" gateway were still standing. It was as if nothing had changed since 1945. Except the residents, of course.

The museum had exhibits of suitcases and eyeglasses, locks of hair, the prisoners' belongings and family photos. It was deathly quiet. There weren't many visitors, but they were all as shocked as we were, and spoke to each other in whispers, as if we were terrified of waking the ghosts of the people who died there in such unthinkably horrific conditions. I felt that I was at the point on the globe where humanity had reached its lowest point.

We visited the crematoria and then walked in the enclosure where the gypsies had lived, before they were all killed. We also went to the labor camp nearby, Buna, where the healthier (or less sick) prisoners were used as slave labor in chemicals factories. We learned that the SS actually made money by hiring the prisoners to German companies making rubber and synthetic oil. When the workers got too slow or too sick, they were beaten to death, gassed or hanged. Amazingly, there were Polish companies still using the old Nazi buildings. Why waste a decent factory building just because it used to be a murder camp, right? Again, there was some chilling historical denial going on.

Nell and I were the only people around in the late afternoon, and when we had finally had enough, we headed back towards the entrance to the camp. The problem was that we were a little lost and had trouble finding our way out of the barbed wire. We got scared and disoriented and wandered along the fences like prisoners trying desperately to find a gap.

Finally, we found a gate, and saw that our taxi driver was driving around, looking for us. He said he'd been worried, and made a joke about the camp not being a great place to spend a long time. We didn't laugh. We noticed he'd kept the meter running just in case we got out.

I felt forced to ask him, "Didn't the Polish people in the town know what was going on here? Didn't they try to stop it?"

"How could you stop the Nazis?" he asked. I had no answer to that.

We drove back to Krakow in silence, and next day, we visited the Jewish ghetto of Krakow and the old synagogue. I guess our driver saw that we were in shock—or maybe he had an attack of guilt—because he suggested that we cut short our tour of the wartime disaster sites, and leave a day early for our next destination, Prague. He wasn't even going to drive us there—we had train tickets. Perhaps he just wanted us to leave Poland. But whatever his reasoning, we jumped at his suggestion. He helped us to change our train tickets, and that was the end of Krakow.

Prague was fun and cheered us up. For a day or two. No more, because only 60 miles away was Theresienstadt, the camp where my friend Johanna's grandparents had been killed. Johanna had been born in Marienbad, a beautiful spa town on the Czech-German border, but she was lucky—her family escaped to New York before the Nazis arrived.

Theresienstadt was a small country town that during the war had been turned into a vastly overcrowded, unsanitary ghetto to hold Jewish prisoners before they were sent on trains to Auschwitz. The old fortress and city buildings that housed the prisoners were still standing.

Theresienstadt was one of the places where the Nazis invited the Red Cross, to show the outside world how well they treated their prisoners. But of course, it was all a sham for the visiting bigwigs, and as soon as the Red Cross left, the Jews were packed into horrendously overcrowded, unsanitary "living" quarters, and the trains were rolling to Auschwitz.

On the bus when we were returning from Theresienstadt to Prague, we were discussing our impressions of the visit with some fellow tourists when a middle-aged Danish visitor got up. He announced to the bus that when the Nazis invaded Denmark, the King went out every day on his horse to show the Germans that the country still belonged to the Danes. Also, he said that very few Danes were killed in Theresienstadt. The Danes, he told us, had sent the Jews to safety in Sweden before the Nazis came. He didn't say it in an arrogant way—he was lamenting the fact that other countries hadn't stood up to the Nazis and protected the Jews.

I told him I agreed. From what I'd seen in Belsen, Riga, Auschwitz and Theresienstadt, during the war plenty of people seem to have accepted the fact that Jews were going to get taken away and used as slave labor, or just murdered. It was the way of the world. They were good at putting up plaques and preserving camps as museums (or even re-using the factory buildings), but they didn't stop it all happening on their doorstep.

It was a hard lesson. Silence, I realized, can kill almost as much as violence. When we keep our eyes and mouths shut in the face of prejudice, we're collaborating in that prejudice.

I was so grateful to be able to hold Nell's hand as we drove away from the horrors of Nazi history.

Chapter 20

Nell Brings Bad News

WHILE MY RELATIONSHIP WITH NELL WAS FLOURISHING, MY father was wilting. He had always been active—it was only after an ice-skating accident in his 70s that his golf swing got weaker. After Mom died, though, he began to suffer from Parkinson's, and a long downhill journey began, both physically and mentally.

I would often go to Boston to see him, and once, in his 80s, I arrived to pick him up outside his apartment building and he leaned into the car and told me,

"Sorry lady, I can't go with you. I'm not as young as I used to be."

He hadn't recognized me. It was sad, but I had to laugh. I thought, who knows what kind of thing he used to get up to—maybe he had a double life like me?

But as time went on, he became more befuddled, and had to have daily home help. For his 90th birthday, Herb and I threw a party for him in a restaurant near his apartment in Boston. At the time he was convinced that he was head over heels in love with his carer, so I begged her to humor him and come along. There weren't many people there, because all of his old friends were dead. And she didn't turn up, so Dad sulked during the whole dinner, and hardly said a word.

Then one day when Dad was on his own, he refused to open the door to Herb, so he had to call the firemen to climb in the window.

"That's the last straw," Herb told me. "I'm putting him in a nursing home."

I couldn't really argue, though I knew Dad would hate it. And as soon as he was in a home, he went into rapid decline. Sometimes the nurses had to tie him to a wheelchair to stop him escaping. Tragic but true.

Finally, he took to his bed and slipped into a semi-coma. The last time I went to see him, he looked as though he was sound asleep, but as soon as I entered the room, he sat up and called out "Diana!" Then he laid back down, closed his eyes, and didn't speak again.

I left him peacefully breathing in his bed, and drove home to New York. When I got there, Nell told me that the nursing home had called to say my father was dead. Maybe my name was his very last word.

As I was driving back to Boston to help make the funeral arrangements, I remembered some advice he gave me early on in life. I'd just split up with someone, and he told me "there's always another pebble on the beach." And I realized it wasn't only true about boyfriends and girlfriends. Because my brother Herb was refusing to help me clear out my father's apartment. He didn't want anything to do with selling the furniture and giving away the clothes to charity. I didn't understand how he could be so heartless towards me and his own father. It hurt, and I consoled myself by thinking that at least I was lucky to have my "other pebble," my rock, Nell, who came up to Boston to be with me during that terrible time. She advised me on which furniture to keep, which antiques to hold on to for myself, and she reminded me how I'd always said that Dad was a calming influence in my life, and had made me stronger. Maybe she was grateful to him, because although he didn't really approve of me being in a relationship with a woman, he had accepted me for who I was and never rejected me or Nell. Unlike my brother, who probably acted tough because he disapproved of my whole lifestyle. I was everything but the submissive wife he thought I ought to be. Whereas my father always wanted me to stand up for myself, even if that meant being with a defrocked nun. Thanks, Dad.

Chapter 21

All Good Nuns
Come to an End

As time went on, Nell seemed to be losing her crazy bohemian streak. She qualified as a teacher and founded the ESL (English as a Second Language) department in the East Hampton school system to accommodate the influx of non-English speaking immigrants.

Meanwhile, I was instrumental in getting Angela accepted into Wellesley College, and we came to an agreement whereby Nell would pay for her education, while I met all our extra-curricular expenses, like our golf club fees and our vacations in Maine and California.

When Angela got married, Nell swore to her that she wouldn't be an interfering mother-in-law, or an interfering grandmother. Meanwhile, she promised me that she and I would have a wonderful life together, traveling and golfing. She would take up painting again—she was very talented—and we would both become famous in our respective careers.

Life was great.

In 2008 Nell retired with a generous pension and moved in with me in New York City. I even bought a condo in Southampton for our golfing weekends. However, something just wasn't right. Nell's daughter Angela was living in Rhode Island, and we would visit, but I felt something was strange. We would arrive there, and Angela would be warm and friendly to Nell: "Hey, Mom! Great to see you!" But all I would receive was a cool "How's it going, D'yan?"

Then the two of them would say they needed time together, and Nell would suggest I spend the day at the coast, or go and have lunch alone somewhere, or try to get myself a game at the local golf club. And sometimes Nell would say she wanted to go visit Angela on her own so that they could have some "quality time." Did she mean that being with me wasn't quality time?

The year Nell retired, she and I went on a trip to the Silk Road in China, and a camel fell on top of me, breaking my leg (hey, it can happen). I came back to New York weighed down with a plaster cast, but Nell didn't seem very caring towards me. Instead of helping me around the apartment, she would tell me to order food from a delivery service. She would go out in the evenings to see friends without me. I offered to struggle down in the elevator and lie on the back seat of the car, but she said it was "too much trouble for me." Too much trouble for her, evidently.

Then she told me Angela and her husband had sent an invitation to go and stay with them.

"Great," I said, "I'm fed up with staying in the apartment. I need to get out."

"They said their house isn't really suitable for someone in a plaster cast," Nell told me. "There are too many stairs and steps. It would be painful for you."

"I've got boxes of painkillers. What I need is fresh air."

"Their bathroom is way too small. You wouldn't be able to wash."

"We'll stay in a motel," I said. "I'll pay."

"But I want to stay with Angela. I'm not going to Rhode Island just to be in a motel."

I got the message. She went alone.

At the beginning of the summer of 2009, Nell relented and let me come along to Rhode Island. My leg was much better, and I was walking again, so she couldn't use the lame bathroom excuse.

The occasion was Nell's niece's wedding, and I was delighted to come along and celebrate, but at the reception, Nell just left me alone with no one to talk to. We arrived in the hotel dining room, and as soon as we had a drink in our hands, she went off to talk to her relatives, and didn't introduce me to anyone. I spent a lonely evening wondering what I'd done to deserve this.

Then, when my birthday came at the end of July, Nell was vacationing with her daughter in Rhode Island and said that she couldn't come back to Southampton to be with me because her son-in-law's birthday was the day before. Which was even more insulting than the old bathroom story.

The very next week, Nell announced that Angela was pregnant and that she was going to leave me. After 25 years together, out of the blue, she was going to move to Rhode Island permanently, and become a full-time nanny while Angela taught school. She had already packed her bags and organized a truck to pick up her belongings from the New York apartment.

I couldn't believe it.

"What happened to the deal we made?" I asked her.

"What deal?"

"Of sharing the future together, of growing old together, traveling the world, and visiting Angela once in a while?"

"I want to grow old with my daughter and grandchild. What's strange about that?"

She was looking cold and detached, like she must have done when she was telling her husband that she was having a baby by one of his friends.

"What's strange about that is that you're forgetting us and everything we've created together."

"Created? We lived together, we traveled—mainly to visit concentration camps, thanks very much. We played golf. But that's all."

"All?" I couldn't believe it. She was erasing history. Why did everyone want to deny what had happened in the past? And these were good things she was denying, not evil things. She was forgetting all the loving times we'd had together. Not to mention all the ways I'd helped her and her daughter. I'd adopted them both as my own family.

Nell seemed impatient to walk out the door. Then she hit me with the bombshell.

"I never really loved you," she said. "I only stayed with you for the perks. The lifestyle. But now I feel like I'm in jail in New York."

I couldn't believe my ears. Jail? We'd visited *real* prisons. Our life together was anything but prison.

"I want to be Rhode Island, she said. "I need to spend time with Angela and the baby."

She walked out.

I was distraught, destroyed. I called Angela, begging her to tell Nell that I loved her and wanted her to come home. Or I could come up to Rhode Island and be with her. Not all day every day of course. I would let them have their quality time.

But Angela said it was no good.

"You just have to accept that Mom doesn't want to be with you anymore. Sorry."

Accept. Acceptance. That word was haunting me. How come people wanted me to accept things when they didn't want to accept me?

THEN, ON TOP OF EVERYTHING, soon afterwards I found out that Nell had started living with another woman in Rhode Island— someone I'd already met. She'd been having an affair. It wasn't all about the baby, after all. She'd been bullshitting me.

I was in total shock, and probably still am.

The last I heard of Nell, she was babysitting for Angela, cleaning her house, doing the errands, cooking and living in a small room next to her family in Rhode Island. Apparently, she lives alone with all her possessions in that one room, and says she has no romantic feelings for anyone anymore.

Once a nun, always a nun—except this one turned into a devil.

Chapter 22

Turning Tragedy to Comedy

BEFORE THINGS WITH NELL TURNED SOUR, SHE HAD BEEN really encouraging with me, and had helped to launch me on a new career.

Up until 2001, I had been making a living as a cabaret singer and pianist. My new "non-ethnic" nose was keeping me in steady work, and I'd now sung Edith Piaf's songs approximately 2001 times more often than she ever did. But then suddenly all the work dried up. The country club parties and private celebrations stopped happening, and my diary was totally empty.

In many ways, so was I. I'd just witnessed first-hand the partial destruction of my home city. On 9/11, when the first plane hit the Twin Towers, I was at home just a mile away. A friend called me: "Are you OK?"

I asked, "Why would I not be?" She told me to turn on the TV.

I saw the pictures, but I couldn't believe it was really happening, so I went up on to the roof of my building and joined the 20 or so of my neighbors gazing downtown. We could see smoke, we could hear sirens, but we still didn't understand.

One tower fell, and one of the neighbors alongside me on the roof said the second one would never go down. Then we watched it collapse. We were stunned into silent horror.

Some of us walked a few blocks to Saint Vincent's Hospital, and asked what was going on. Details were hazy, but people were talking about a terrorist attack on the city. Using airplanes.

Some of the doctors and nurses started heading south towards the disaster zones, following the fire trucks that were speeding past, their sirens blaring. Others waited with us outside the hospital, looking towards the plume of dust and smoke billowing up into the air where the towers had been.

A few cars and trucks emerged, dirty, looking as though they'd been through a sandstorm. They were smothered in some kind of grey-brown dust, and their wipers had cleared two semicircular spaces on the windshields. Plenty of people were walking away, scared. The subways had stopped so passengers had to get out and use their feet.

We waited and waited, doctors, nurses, paramedics and we ordinary citizens, and nothing came. No ambulances. It was as if everyone had died in the towers. There were no casualties to be treated, no one to be saved. In a way, that was worse than seeing lots of injured people arrive.

THE EVENTS OF THAT DAY tore me to pieces. Like the concentration camps, the violence of this attack seemed to be irrational, needless, and aimed at innocents. What had the people who worked in those towers done to deserve death by burning, suffocation or falling from such a great height?

Why did the passengers on those planes deserve to die? Why would anyone want to topple two beautiful towers which, in their own way, were works of art? That old question "Why, why, why?" was haunting me again.

Well, people have put forward all sorts of complex geopolitical explanations for 9/11, as well as some crazy conspiracy theories, but to me it represented nothing more complex than the deliberate destruction of a part of my home, and the premeditated killing of innocent people just like me. It sent my thoughts rushing back to the wanton destruction of part of my family sixty years earlier. I plummeted into depression.

And of course, I wasn't the only one to be deeply depressed, because, like I said, the partying all stopped. And with it, so did my work.

Suddenly there was so much negativity in my life, in all New Yorkers' lives, that I realized how much I needed positivity, in the form of laughter. I decided to become a comedian. I had to make people laugh again. Maybe make myself laugh, too.

The first reactions I got from friends and neighbors were negative: "You're too old!" (I was 67). "Audiences will just heckle you!" "Comedy shows are on too late at night. You'll fall asleep!"

The only person being at all positive was Nell. She reminded me that I could be really funny when I was playing piano in the bars. Pretty often, I would accidentally knock my music off the stand, and have to banter while I picked it all up and put it back into some kind of order. Sometimes this would take a few minutes—as long as the average stand-up's slot in a comedy club. Nell said she was sure I could turn the improvised bantering into a comedy act.

So I summoned up all my courage, and talked to the owner of Caroline's Comedy Club in Manhattan. Her name was—you guessed it—Caroline, and she was one of the friendly people at my golf club, one of the members who actually wanted to lunch with me now and then. She didn't offer to put me on stage directly, but she did put me in touch with a comedy coach.

Here again, I got more negativity.

"Are you sure about this?" the coach asked me. "Lots of people think they're funny, but they can't do it on stage."

"I do it on stage already." I explained about the banter. "I get laughs," I told her.

"But that's just while the audience is waiting for you to play another song. Standing up there purely to get laughs is a different thing."

"Well I want to try it."

"OK, we'll give it a try." Boy, was she a great motivator.

She told me to go home and write as many funny things about my life as I could think of. I wrote them all down. Things that had happened to me, things people said, accidents, misunderstandings, eccentric characters, my mother's yelling, my father's trick with the Christmas tree under the car, my choir teacher revealing he was Jewish, my husband taking me to Quebec instead of Paris, pages of stuff.

When I brought them to the comedy coach, she read them all and said, "Not funny, not funny, not funny."

"I can do some comedy songs, too," I said.

"Comedians don't do songs. You have to decide whether you're a comedian or a musician."

I told her that early on in my career, when I used to sing in the Catskills, I used to spend a lot of time backstage with the stars of the shows, who would usually be stand-up comedians. And one of them told me that no matter what shtick he did, he always went down better if he ended his act with a song. I thought that was a good showbiz lesson, even if I was taught it back in the 1960s.

"Modern comedians don't sing," she said. "Does Seinfeld sing? No. End of story."

But I stuck to my guns.

"I'm sure I could do some funny songs between gags."

"But you can't be stuck behind a piano. You've got to be out front, at the microphone, face-to-face with your audience."

I had an idea. "I've got an old ukulele. I used to play it when I was a teenager. Couldn't I bring that on stage?"

She grudgingly said OK.

We started trying to develop some of my stories into jokes and funny anecdotes with a punchline, with me doing snippets of funny songs like "Make 'Em Laugh" from *Singin' in the Rain*. But my coach still didn't think I was very funny.

Then one day she suddenly asked me: "Hey, are you gay?"

I was dumbfounded, but finally said, "Sort of. I live with a defrocked nun." (This was before Nell and I broke up.)

My coach laughed.

"A defrocked nun? Why didn't you mention this before?"

"I thought it's a bit private. And we get a lot of disapproval. I want everyone to like me when I get up on stage. I don't want to alienate anyone in the audience."

On the contrary, she said. There was an active gay comedy scene in NYC, and I could get a lot of work with gay material. Everyone in those audiences would love me. There would be absolutely no problem of alienation.

For a week I thought hard about all this, because I had never talked publicly about my confused sexuality, and never gave even a hint about it when performing. And I finally decided that I hadn't become famous being straight, so what did I have to lose by trying a new sexual orientation in my career?

We put together a short set with a song, and a couple of weeks later I did my first comedy slot of eight minutes. My opening lines went like this:

"I've been in show business for a long time. I was playing the piano at five years old, and when I was fourteen, I asked my parents for a guitar for my birthday. What I got was this ukulele. I said, 'But I wanted a guitar.'

They said, 'We know, but guitars are for boys, and you're kind of like a boy, but smaller. So, we got you a ukulele.' Yes, even then they knew I was AC/DC."

I then sang a parody version of "Thank Heaven for Little Girls"–"Thank Heaven for Senior Sex." And the crowd laughed.

And that first laugh, that first time that people reacted to my script as I'd hoped they would, with genuine laughter, was magic. It was a shot of adrenaline to my system, a massive injection of positivity. When I came off stage after eight laughter-filled minutes, to loud and happy applause, I felt as though I was surfing a wave of new hope, or more exactly as if I was the golf ball soaring off the tee towards a hole in one. Uplifted was not the word for what I was feeling. I was flying.

I performed the same act a few more times, and each time it went down very well. Pretty soon I was working different clubs, and I started opening with a new line, inspired by the gay cowboy movie *Brokeback Mountain*:

"Like most dykes (oops, sorry, gay women), I love golf. The members of my club are very friendly, but they're really conservative, especially about gay parenting. They do not believe gays can be fit parents. Well, I've never seen anything but great parenting from gay couples. They're always singing to their kids..."

"Oh, give me a home where the buffalo roam
Where the deer and the antelope are gay
Where seldom is heard a homophobic word,
And now we know how the cowboys do play
Homo, homo on the range...."

I WOULD TELL THE AUDIENCE: "I loved *Brokeback Mountain*. I've been asked to star in a sequel, *Bad Back Mountain*. It's about two elderly gay cowgirls who have lots of hot sex and then spend the next six weeks in a chiropractor's office."

Then I would do a cowgirl song:

"She'll be comin' round the mountain when she comes...
She'll be comin' sooner than later
She just got a new vibrator
You can hear her all over the mountain when she comes."

The reactions were wonderful. These gay audiences accepted me for who I was. Better than that—they accepted an *exaggerated* version of who I was. Off stage I would never talk about having a loud orgasm thanks to a vibrator. In these clubs, though, I could say what I wanted. And I realized that this kind of laughter, where the audience is laughing with you, not at you, where they sympathize with your problems and share your amusement at the world, is the most sincere, spontaneous sort of acceptance. As they laughed, the audiences were saying, yes, I know what she is talking about, I am with her. Thinking this gave my confidence in myself as a person, and who I was, a massive boost.

THE GAY SHOWS WENT ABSOLUTELY fantastic every time, but I also wanted to get booked to do slots in non-gay clubs. I went to a writer, and he said, "Gay is great in gay clubs, but to broaden your appeal, why not do bisexual comedy? Nobody does that."

We put together an act with a lot of bisexual jokes, and I finished the set by asking the audience:

"I was confused about my sexuality even as a child, and who do you go to when you're confused? Your Mom." Then I'd sing....

"When I was just a little girl, I asked my mother, what will I be?

Will I like women, will I like men, or something in between?

Que sera, she said, you'll love men I guarantee,

If not, you'll go to therapy,

Que sera, sera.

So, I did the wedding thing, my new rich husband, his name was Lee

He didn't thrill me, he didn't charm me, I liked his niece, Marie.

Que sera, he said, who do you choose, me or Marie?

I said, I like you both, you see, so let's do a three.

Que sera, sera,

So, we did a three.

Now after many, many years, I still don't know which team I'm on.

I love the boys. I love the girls. I confess honestly.

Que sera, sera, human sexuality, it's all such a mystery.

I just love sex, you see,

Que sera, sera..."

This version of my comedy act was even more liberating. Probably because it was more honest about who I was. I told the audience:

"I've kept this secret about my bisexuality for the last 50 years, so this really is huge for me to tell a room full of strangers. It would be scary, but my girlfriend's happy, my shrink is happy, and all the people I was afraid to tell are dead."

And that part of the act was 100% true.

I was well and truly launched in my new direction. I was being honest about my true self, and audiences of complete strangers were accepting me for it. Their laughter was better therapy than anything you can get from someone who hires out their couch for two hundred dollars an hour.

My new career as a comedian had taken off and was curing me of plenty of my demons. But there was some residual darkness that still needed to be cleared out of my system.

Chapter 23

Hello to Berlin

IN 2011, WHILE TRAVELING IN EUROPE, I MET A COUPLE FROM Augsburg, Germany. They invited me to visit them.

I asked where Augsburg was.

"Not far from Munich," they said.

"Great," I said. "I really want to go to Dachau concentration camp—maybe we could we go there together?"

To be fair to them, after their initial shock, they agreed, so I was off to Augsburg, a lovely city that had been devastated during World War Two by allied bombing, but where the beautiful synagogue was still standing. For once, the bombs must have known what they were doing.

On the third day of my visit, we went to Dachau. It was just ten miles or so from the city of Augsburg, and right near a charming little country village. I was beginning to get the picture. All these terrible places were near towns and villages, not far away from civilization, even if they were masked by trees. They weren't secrets at all. They had been built and operated out in the open.

Dachau was huge, and still had its barracks, torture centers and crematoria. I walked around the museum, which documented the full horror of the place, where—for example—experiments were carried out to see how long it took prisoners to die in the cold. There were photos of the prisoners, naked, being put into the tanks of iced water, their empty gaze at the camera expressing the impossibility of what was happening to them. The idea, the photo captions said, was to discover how long Nazi pilots could survive after parachuting or crashing into the sea in winter. I disagreed—the idea was to kill Dachau prisoners in (literally) cold blood.

After our visit to the camp, we stopped off in the pretty village of Dachau. We had dinner in a café, where a group of older German people were enjoying themselves, talking, drinking and singing.

They must have been children during the war, I thought. They were dressed like locals, with their check shirts and green jackets. I wondered what they knew about the camp while it was in use. I wanted to ask them. I was pretty sure my question would have stopped their singing.

LATER THAT SAME YEAR, BACK in New York, I read about a new exhibition of German propaganda in the history museum in Berlin, so I decided to visit the German capital for the first time. Almost as soon as I got there, a taxi driver called Bernd, who spoke English perfectly, suggested that he could be my personal guide. I agreed, and the next morning at 9 am, I was standing up to my knees in snow in the center of Berlin, with him explaining how the first city had been built here by the Romans. (I wasn't sure about the historical accuracy of that. Maybe he'd got Berlin mixed up with Rome, but I didn't argue.)

We went to the history museum and saw the Propaganda Exhibit. It showed how, after 1918, the extreme right in Germany had begun a campaign through posters, newspapers and radio to blame the Communists and Jews for losing the First World War. When the Nazis came to power, the propaganda show went mainstream.

Most of the explanations were in German, so when I couldn't understand what I was seeing, I asked Bernd or another German person to explain. All the other visitors were German, and when they weren't talking to me, it was so quiet you could hear a pin drop. I have a feeling that most of them had never seen an exhibition like this before, and they were a little stunned by the scale of the propaganda machine that had taken over their country in the 1930s and 1940s.

I asked Bernd to take me to any other places in and around Berlin that dealt with the Nazi persecution of the Jews, and the following day he took me to Wannsee, where in 1942, Heydrich, Eichmann and the top brass of the SS decided on the "final solution." They decided that people like my relatives in Riga were going to be murdered. They listed all the Jews living in Europe, including countries they hadn't invaded, like Britain, Ireland and Spain, and discussed ways of killing millions of people. Madness doesn't come much madder, but they acted as if it was all perfectly rational.

The conference took place in a palace (that they call a "villa") which enjoyed a superb view of the lake. An idyllic place to plan genocide. We visited it, and I was able to look into the faces of the twenty or thirty bureaucrats who sat down to discuss the fate of my relatives, and, who knows, my own fate if we had lost the war. The photos showed a dull-looking bunch of nobodies, some of them trying to look important in their Nazi uniforms. But then only a bunch of nobodies, losers and disturbed minds would agree to participate in the planning of genocide.

Bernd walked around the museum with me, learning as much as I did, and shaking his head in disgust. Of course, whenever we were together, the meter of his taxi was running, but he was always excellent and helpful company.

AFTER LEAVING GERMANY THAT TIME, I found out that Bernd hadn't showed me everything that would have interested me. I saw that the Sachsenhausen concentration camp was only 22 miles from the center of Berlin.

So, in 2017, I went back, and this time it was off to Sachsenhausen in Bernd's taxi—with the meter running as always. We got there from the center of town in only about 20 minutes, and sure enough, confirming my ideas about these places, the camp was set in a forest, next to a picturesque village.

What was different about Sachsenhausen, though, was that the center of the camp where they did roll calls had a huge oval track around the edge. The guards made the inmates run around it for hours in shoes that the manufacturers were trying out before putting them into full production. They didn't care if the shoes were the right size. They just wanted to know how the leather stood up to wear and tear. Without caring about the wear and tear on the prisoners. It was similar to what went on at the factories in Buna. The SS were working with private businesses, hiring out their prisoners as workers and guinea pigs, killing them when they stopped being economically viable.

At Sachsenhausen, there were no barracks left, but some buildings had been turned into museums which told the whole gory story. In one room, the prisoners were led in so that their height could be measured. But when they stood with their back against the wall, an SS man behind the wall shot them in the neck. In the end, though, this method was considered to be too time-consuming, so the guards just dug a mass grave (or rather, got the prisoners to dig it) and then made their victims stand on the edge of the pit so they fell in when they were shot. All very efficient.

On the way back into Berlin, Bernd and I stopped at a cute market in a charming little suburb, full of care-free Germans buying healthy food and drinking beer at a timeless-looking outdoor pub. For much of the war, it was probably just the same. For the prisoners along the road a mile or two, it would have been so near and yet so far.

BY NOW I WAS ON a mission. I needed to see these camps on German soil, where the people who had voted for the Nazis (don't forget they won an election) would have been able to see the direct human results of their government's insane policies. The question I had been asking myself—"Why, why, why?"—was still haunting me. And the silence and denial from the Germans of the period were proving themselves more and more to be part of the answer. I know that has been said before, but I was educating myself, finding my own evidence.

Next up, in 2018, I went to Ravensbrück, a concentration camp especially for women. Though I doubt that they were thrilled about such favoritism.

It was built 56 miles north of Berlin, only a short train ride away. Bernd and I set off there (he was a friend now, rather than a taxi driver) and about 45 minutes later we found ourselves in a quaint German village, set on a picturesque lake. Surprise, surprise, the camp was right next to the village, spread out through the woodland on the other side of the lake. We took a two-minute taxi ride, passing beautiful houses that had been the homes of the commandant and the head SS officers based at the camp.

When I went inside one of the houses, I got a shock. It looked just like the homes that were built in the 1930s where I grew up in Newton, Massachusetts. Perfect suburban havens, with a living room and kitchen downstairs, and a second floor with the bedrooms and bathroom. It was so similar to my old family home that I couldn't believe it. Something so ordinary and homely, but occupied by monsters.

The rest of camp had been destroyed except for one big building that contained the museum and the place where they shot the women prisoners against the wall.

Towards the end of the war, they built crematoria to get rid of the prisoners who were pouring in from the camps in the east that were being overtaken by the Russians. All the time, the prisoners who were being tortured and killed could look across the lake at the church spires and quaint houses in the village. And presumably the people in the village could see, hear, and even smell, what was going on opposite.

Bernd and I rode back on the train to Berlin. At first, we sat in silence, then he spoke up. I think he suspected what I was thinking about the Germans who had let all these horrors be committed on their behalf, because he began to explain.

"My parents and grandparents never talked about this period," he said.

"I know why," I said.

"I don't know what they did during the war." He said it like a confession. "I'm very interested to learn about what happened in the camps. Everyone should visit them."

I thanked him for saying that, and for accompanying me on these harrowing trips. It felt good to be partners in observing crimes.

A FEW MONTHS AFTER MY trip to Ravensbrück, I saw a documentary about Himmler. In it, he visited a concentration camp that I had never heard of. It was called Mauthausen, in Austria. On my next visit to Europe, instead of bothering Bernd, I took a 12-hour train ride to the city of Linz, which was only 15 miles from the camp.

I found a room in a comfortable hotel on a beautiful old Austrian square. This was the town where Hitler grew up, the place he wanted to turn into a cultural capital, with a museum for all the art he had stolen from the countries he invaded. So it was fitting that it should have had its very own Nazi concentration camp nearby. They were an integral part of Nazi culture, after all.

I took a taxi with a young driver, and after a half hour driving along the wide, peaceful Danube valley, we passed through a beautiful village of clean, pastel-colored buildings and turned up a hill. Two minutes later, *voilà,* the camp.

It had started to drizzle and, dripping and cold, I looked around, all alone at nine in the morning.

The camp was built on a cliff overlooking a granite quarry. I had seen in the documentary that the prisoners had to go down to the bottom of the pit, load a granite block on to their back, and then walk up a steep stairway in rows of four, tightly packed in a column, one line behind the other. If someone stumbled on the way up, he fell back on top of the others below him, and they all toppled, in a domino effect.

Once they reached the top, the men dropped their blocks of granite, and the weakest prisoners were sent to the edge of the cliff. Other prisoners would be ordered to push them over the edge, or they would be pushed over themselves.

The barracks in the camp were still standing, and there was a good, informative museum. I listened to a tape of a local woman saying that the Nazi guards would come down to the village on Saturday nights, when there were dances, and everybody had a wonderful time. The message seemed to be that the monsters were really nice men when they weren't torturing prisoners.

I also learned that the trains stopped at the village and that the sick and malnourished prisoners were marched up the mountain right in front of the villagers. Some of the locals even had jobs at the camp. In short, everybody knew what went on in Mauthausen. To me, this made the experience all the more shocking. Here, there was not just indifference to suffering, there was active participation.

The one bright spot of the visit was a group of Austrian high-school students who were visiting the camp with their teacher. I spoke to her and she told me that the region's schools were trying to educate younger generations by showing them places like this. So there was hope that it wouldn't happen again.

After Linz, I went on to Vienna, where I visited Sigmund Freud's home. I learned that he was lucky—as a famous man, he was helped to escape from Austria after the *Anschluss* (the annexation of Austria by Germany) in 1938, along with his wife and daughter. His sisters were less fortunate. Although they were in their late 70s and early 80s, four of them were sent to concentration camps and killed.

IN EARLY 2020, I WENT back to Germany, this time to visit Buchenwald, the concentration camp just outside the city of Weimar, the home of Germany's national poet, Goethe. Proof that despite their claims to patriotism, the Nazis had zero respect for their country's heritage.

This time, I had to coax Bernd along by paying his expenses. We took a two-hour train ride from Berlin to Weimar, then an eight-minute taxi ride up a mountain. The camp was in a huge forest only ten miles from the city.

The cutely-named Buchenwald (it means beech forest) looked out over a beautiful view of fields, trees and mountains. The commandant's house and some guards' homes were left standing, but the barracks had all been destroyed, and there were only huge rectangular mounds to show where the prisoners had been housed.

For me, the most moving building was the one that was presented to the prisoners as a medical center. When they entered, they were ordered to take off all their clothes, go into the next room, which was full of glass cabinets containing medical instruments, and told to stand against a wall to be measured. It was the same trick as at Sachsenhausen. Behind the wall was a guard with a gun, who shot the prisoner in the head. By now, though, my thinking had progressed—or maybe regressed—so far that I thought to myself, well, at least they never knew what hit them, unlike the people who were starved or beaten to death, used in medical experiments, or who smelled the first clouds of gas seeping into their "shower" room. But then I blocked out that thought—it felt like resignation, or even acceptance of the mass murder that had been committed, as if shooting a man in the head through a hole in the wall was somehow less of a murder than gassing him. No, murder was murder, genocide was genocide, and subtle differences in the technique didn't mean a thing.

Buchenwald was the camp that my mother had told me about when I was a child. This was where Ilse Koch had earned her nickname "the witch of Buchenwald", because it was said that she killed some of the prisoners who had tattoos so that she could make their skin into lampshades. But in a way, what I learned in the museum at Buchenwald was even more horrific, if that was possible. I read that the first commandant of the camp, Karl-Otto Koch, and his wife Ilse had actually been arrested by the Nazis. Not for cruelty, though. Karl-Otto had been using the prisoners as labor to make money for himself, instead of passing on the profits to the Nazi state. Karl-Otto was shot by firing squad, and Ilse was put in prison for four years. It shows the Nazis' priorities—the corrupt commandant was shot, the psychopathic murderess got four years.

Buchenwald was the first concentration camp I'd heard about, and I decided that it would be the last I visited. I've seen enough evidence of the horror. I've understood enough about denial.

But there's one more reason why I won't visit any more of the German camps. While I was in Weimar, the far right won a regional election there. The neo-Nazis were voted back in. Call it ignorance, denial, forgetfulness, but it just proves the old adage: what goes around comes around. And I'm not going back.

Chapter 24

It Ain't Over Till the Old Lady Dies

MY MOTTO IS THE OLDEST THEATRE CLICHÉ OF ALL—THE SHOW must go on. I've always tried to live up to it. In 2019, at the age of 85, I was in Paris when I started feeling breathless. Suddenly I couldn't walk ten yards without stopping to pant like an exhausted horse. A doctor told me that one of my arteries was 85% blocked and I needed an immediate operation to put in a stent. France is a very efficient country, so only a few hours later I was listening to an anesthetist counting down: "dix, neuf, huit, sept ..."

When I got out of the hospital two days later, a friend called me up and said, "I hope you're taking it easy."

I reassured him, "Don't worry, I'll be in bed all day. The show tonight isn't until 9 pm."

Yes, I'd agreed to perform a comedy slot in a Paris club just 48 hours after having heart surgery.

My friend begged me not to go out: "What's the point of doing an eight-minute slot in some basement in Paris, to a bunch of French-speakers who will only understand half of what you're saying, and who will probably put a fake euro coin in the hat as they leave the club?"

He was right, but the point was, and still is, that I need to be on stage, performing, or I just don't feel alive. What's the use of getting your arteries scrubbed out if you're not going to use your new lease of life to perform?

So, I did the show—exhausted, unsteady on my feet, anxious that I might drop dead—and I'm sure the audience's laughter did me as much good as the operation. I felt as if the crowd had given me a collective shot of amphetamines. Being on stage again was the confirmation that I had survived.

I STILL LOVE DOING THOSE slots in comedy clubs. They're short-but-sweet rushes of adrenaline and laughter-induced joy. But I also like to perform longer acts, which is why I have written or co-written a whole string of one-woman shows.

My first, *Chasing the Sunlight*, happened in 2011. I was going through a tough period, still getting over Nell dumping me, and my comedy coach said, "Why not write about it?" At the same time, I found out about a theater that wanted new performers, so as soon as I had written a couple of pages, I sent them to the director, and I was accepted to do a one-hour show.

I was ecstatic and scribbled away like crazy so I could be ready in time. This wasn't going to be a straight comedy show, I decided. It would be more of an up-and-down emotional ride, with much stronger sentiments than I put into the comedic version of my life story.

The theater was a beautiful venue holding more than a hundred people. Of course, I wanted to be sure I'd fill it, so

I invited everybody I knew, and just to be on the safe side, I told them that there would be food and wine afterwards.

Thanks to the promise of refreshments, I managed to fill the theater, and I gave the audience an hour or more of stories about the good and bad times with Nell and my ultimate heartbreak, and I sang songs, accompanying myself on the ukulele and the piano. It wasn't comedy, exactly, more of a bittersweet (much more bitter than sweet) memoir.

Bizarrely, for once I was petrified on stage. I'd performed in public countless times, but I had never done a long, solo speaking show before. Singing for an hour, with a bit of chit-chat between songs, is not so hard. I now found it relatively straightforward to tell well-rehearsed gags, even when I was joking about my private life. But this one-woman show was much tougher. It was an exposé, a confessional, an often serious re-telling of the whole truth about my life. I was scared the audience might be embarrassed or disapprove.

But I was a huge hit! The audience accompanied me on every difficult step of my lonely trip through a doomed love story, and supported me with cheers, laughs, and huge applause at the end. (Unless, of course, they were clapping because they knew it was almost time for the food and wine.)

In any case, my one-woman show career was launched.

THE FOLLOWING YEAR, I DECIDED to make things even clearer, and wrote a show called *I Married a Nun*. In this, I went even further into the most painful details of my life with Nell, in stories, songs, comedy and pathos. It was such a hit in NYC that I took it to the Orlando Festival and performed to a full house of Floridians every night. Again, I felt accepted, and enjoyed the audiences' love and sympathy. And people were obviously intrigued by all the things you could do with a nun.

NEXT UP, I DID A show with a positive feel at last. I had just met someone new, a woman called Betty, and I was having a fantastic time, and wanted to share it with the rest of the world. So, I called the show *My Pussy Is Purring Again*. You can't get clearer than that, right?

This time, not only did I sing and play the piano, I also played the trumpet and the glockenspiel. I performed the show in New York and Orlando, but I didn't get great crowds. I quickly realized why. It wasn't that I was blowing my own trumpet (literally) about being happy, it was the title. It was just plain pornographic. You can be provocative, but not *that* provocative.

It was an important lesson, and one that I'm always re-minded of when I do comedy shows and see young comedians who give the audience a solid stream of f-words. Cursing might shock the crowd into laughter at first, but after a while it's just boring. Provocation needs to be subtle.

Incidentally, the happiness with Betty didn't last much longer than the show itself. After a few months she broke up with me because I wouldn't pay for her golf lessons. Turned out she saw me as the nineteenth hole. (Sorry about that joke, but you don't *always* need to be subtle.)

* * *

THEN IN 2014 IT WAS as if my own body wanted to break up with me. I was diagnosed with lung cancer. I started having chemo sessions, which made me feel nauseous and exhausted. But of course, I had to keep on performing. So I put together a show called *Memories of Paris*, in which I spent most of the time sitting at the piano. Less tiring that way.

I performed my favorite Parisian songs, the ones I'd done in cabarets when I was pretending to be French. These were tunes made famous by Piaf, Juliette Greco, Charles Aznavour, Jacques Brel, the Montmartre singer Patachou and Jacqueline Francois (the glamour girl who sang the famous "Mademoiselle de Paris"). And I used to fix the dates of the performances so they were between chemo sessions, after the effects of each treatment had worn off. My diary would be: chemo, wait three weeks, showtime, chemo, and so on. Performing kept me sane—and alive.

ONCE I'D PULLED THROUGH MY cancer, I went back to my coach and talked about broadening my horizons. Together we came up with the idea for a new show about my travels all over the world. We called it *A Broad Abroad*.

Of course, it wasn't just about picturesque views, golf courses and jet lag. The show was about my erotic adventures across the planet, and the theme song was "Toucha Toucha Me" from the movie *The Rocky Horror Show*. This time I hired a pianist to perform with me, so I could really run around the whole stage as I spoke and sang. I also spent quite a lot of time rolling around on the floor. My old mime teachers would have been proud of me.

Why so much rolling? Well, mostly because the show contained lots of stories about massages.

My favorite was the rubdown I got in Petra, Jordan. It made for some great mime scenes. I was traveling in Jordan with a group, and when we checked into the hotel by the famous stone temple in Petra, a guy at the reception desk said that for an extra $35, we could have a Turkish bath before dinner. We all said, "No, no, no! We're Americans. We don't like to be bathed by people we don't know!"

Later on, I walked past the entrance to the baths, and a gentleman said, "Why not come in and enjoy our Turkish bath? If you don't tell the front desk, I'll only charge you $25."

I went in and he gave me a towel and said, "Take off all your clothes." It reminded me of those Parisian parties of so long ago. I wondered what I was getting myself into. I hoped it was something more than soap and water. One promising sign—the towel he gave me was about the size of a wash cloth.

Then a tall, handsome, young man appeared, and led me by the hand into a beautiful cupola-domed room with marble benches and alcoves. The place was empty except for us. Ahmed, that was his name, sat me on a marble bench as a gush of steam shot out in full force and I was suddenly towel-less. I was completely nude with the most gorgeous man I'd ever seen, who now started massaging... my hands.

I felt a burst of passion, immediately followed by a heavy dose of guilt. He was 25, I was 76. It sounds like a math problem. Well, one thing I remembered from school: 25 can go into 76 a lot more than 76 goes into 25. I hoped Ahmed would do the math.

Another problem: he was Syrian, I was Jewish. Could we achieve harmony between the two rivals in the Middle East?

He went and got a large bucket.

"Lie down," he told me. "Mud."

(And in my show, this was where I would lie down on my stomach on the stage.)

Ahmed massaged me all over with hot mud, then soaped me up from head to toe. Then he told me, "Turn over".

Turn over? I flipped over faster than a pancake at IHOP on Mother's Day.

(On stage, it was the cue for a rapid rollover on to my back.)

Ahmed's hands slid all over my breasts and inner thighs. I couldn't believe it. I'd always heard about the proverbial "happy ending" of massages, but I never dreamed I would be getting one like this.

(On stage, cue lots of trembling on the floor.)

Then suddenly he said, "Now you rest." And he left.

And I thought, Rest? I don't need rest! I need you to finish me! Give me that soap!

A BROAD ABROAD WAS A whole collection of stories like that, and it was a big hit with New Yorkers so I decided to take it to the 2016 Edinburgh Festival for a month-long run.

I had a blast in Scotland. I played golf during the day, hired a pianist for my show in the evening, and performed with my ukulele in the crowded bars around midnight. I got a big write-up in the Edinburgh newspaper and pulled in pretty good crowds.

However, I hit a problem with the older ladies who came to my show. They were grey-haired types, but ten or 20 years younger than me, and when I would meet them after the show, they practically called me a liar.

"You can't really be 83!"

"You didn't really do all that outrageous stuff!"

"You invented it all to get a laugh!"

I assured them that it was all true, and told them, "Go to Jordan and get a massage! It's not too late. If you're in your sixties or seventies, now's the perfect time to start having some guilt-free fun."

But even the ones who giggled weren't convinced. In any case, they definitely weren't ready to go around the world looking for a happy ending. These women thought that it was wrong somehow to treat themselves to a little gratuitous pleasure. Even the single women and the widows told me, "oh no, I could never do that!"

I began to wonder if I wasn't a bit weird for wanting to do so myself. Definitely not too old, but maybe too immoral, too self-centered, in a way too free-thinking. Perhaps that's why I never fit in anywhere, I thought, because I don't share other people's values. They can tell that I just might do anything, anytime, in the name of fun. I would never do anything dangerous or hurtful to anyone else, of course, but to other people I might seem like a potential embarrassment. They might be sitting with me in a fancy restaurant—at the golf club, for example—having a normal conversation, then suddenly I'll start describing the massage I just got. Could it be that, even at my age, I'm some kind of *femme fatale?*

WELL, TALKING OF *FEMMES FATALES*, in 2017 I decided it was time to head back to France to perform, this time trying something new. I had a new show called *The Cougar*, which, as its title suggests, was about getting it on with younger men. As I say in the show, I didn't have much choice: I had to go with younger men because the older ones were dead. And if they weren't dead yet, getting it on with me would probably kill them.

This time, I decided to maximize my chances of hitting it big by doing the act both in English and in French. I'd heard that there was an active English-language comedy scene in Paris, and that comedy clubs were just getting popular in French too.

Of course, there have been French stand-up comedians forever, but until recently there were comparatively few of them, and most of them did sketches, often using "comedy" voices and "comic" characters. Friends told me that a lot of the famous French comedians just made fun of other people, pointing out how stupid everyone was. They hadn't been doing the Anglo-American thing of standing up on stage and having a laugh at *yourself*.

So, I decided that I would be one of the people introducing the French to this different style of comedy.

It all started off pretty well.

Firstly, as the most experienced comic in the small clubs, I was usually top of the bill. Back in New York, I'd usually been the opening act—not because I was an unknown, but because the kindly producers knew I liked to go home and get to bed early. But in Paris, I was happy to go on last, because no matter how late it was, I always had to wait until the end of the show, or even later. Our fee would come from passing the hat—or rather, the producer holding out the hat as the audience filed out. And the comedians had to hang around to make sure the cash was counted correctly. Producers can be really bad at math when it suits them.

It was all good fun, and very exotic-feeling, but there were two problems with all this.

First, I quickly learnt that just because Parisians come along to an English-language comedy show, it doesn't mean they understand English.

Sure, they've watched a few seasons of *The Crown* on TV, probably with subtitles, but that doesn't help them understand a New Yorker talking about her sex life, live on stage.

After a few shows in English where some of my sure-fire lines failed to get a laugh, I realized that I had to make things simpler for the audiences. So, I cut out most of the wordplay. No verbal asides, no cultural references. I stuck to the shocking stories, pepped up here and there with a little of my old mime techniques, and they loved it. But whenever I got subtle, they got lost.

All in all, my English act wasn't going great except when there was a big group of real English-speakers in the audience, to get the laughs coming on cue.

The second problem was that I'd had my act translated into French by a translator. He was good, but translating comedy isn't like translating an instruction booklet, or even a novel. You can't translate a joke literally: "Why do you never hear psychoanalysts go to the bathroom? Because the p is silent." Forget it, the translation won't mean a thing.

Now, I don't tell jokes (especially old jokes like that), I tell stories, but the principle is the same. You can't translate funny dialogue literally, you have to adapt it, tell it in a French way, using French wordplay, if you want the French to laugh. They're a very verbal nation.

It was the same with my comedy songs. *The Cougar* had some great new parody songs, and my American writer, Eric Kornfeld, had done a brilliant job on them. But translating a song into another language means rewriting it totally. So I needed to find someone who could write new French song words for me. And funny ones, too.

My French act needed a total revamp. But where would I find someone who could write jokes and song words in French, while fully understanding the original English version?

I was in luck. In October 2017, I went along to a small basement comedy club to do an eight-minute slot on a bill with five or six other English-language comedians. I performed some shtick from my *Cougar* act, including the theme song from the show, then went and sat at the bar to wait for my share of the producer's hat.

At the bar, I got talking to an elegant Anglo-French couple. It turned out they were both published writers. She was French and he was British. Both of them were totally bilingual. Stephen Clarke was a friend of one of the British comics, and had come along to watch him.

"Great songs," he told me, "the words are very clever. Shame it's such a small club." We were in a place that held maximum twenty people on a good night.

"Thanks," I said, "I'd love to do them in a bigger club, one of the French-language places, but my act doesn't work in French. I've had it translated but even I can tell it's just not funny. Especially the songs. Sometimes they don't even rhyme!"

Stephen was sympathetic. "It's the same for my books. They've been translated into lots of languages I can't speak. I can read the French and German translations, and sometimes I have to tell the translators, 'No, you didn't understand—that was a *joke*.' And I have to explain the gag so they can find an equivalent that works in the language. When I'm lucky, the Czech, Polish or Russian translator writes me an email—'was that serious or was it a joke?' or 'what does the pun in that chapter title refer to?' Translating comedy is a tough job."

"You're right," I agreed. "My French translator knows that my act is all jokes, but still can't get it."

Then Stephen's partner, Natacha, leaned over and said, "Stephen could translate your jokes into French. And he writes songs, so he could do those too."

"Seriously?" I said.

Stephen said, "It would be fun to try." He told me to send him the whole act, including the songs, with their melodies, and he would look at it.

I emailed the act and sent him some links to my performances online, and thought I might never hear from him again, but lo and behold, about two weeks later I got an email containing a file with rewrites of my French punchlines and translations of the songs. He'd said it had been a fun exercise for him, so he'd just gone ahead and done it all. He hadn't tried to translate literally, he'd *adapted*. Which was exactly what I wanted to hear.

I didn't understand some of the slang he'd used, and some of the lines that I could understand were more vulgar than the material I do in English. I'm more risqué than graphic. For example, in the act there was a song about being a cougar, with the lines:

"I ain't sixteen, not a beauty queen,

My eyes are baggin' and my skin is saggin'."

And Stephen's new French version was:

"Pour les jeunes mecs, je suis le rêve,

J'ai toutes mes dents, mais elles s'enlèvent."

Literally, in English that would be: "For young guys, I'm a dream / I have all my teeth, but I can take them out." Which is not at all a literal translation of the original English song, right? It's a rewrite on the same theme.

The French lines were much more vulgar than the English version, but a French friend said she thought that the new words were really funny, and that the tone was just right, because the French love to be shocked by that kind of vulgarity. My friend also explained all the slang words for me, so I would know what I was singing about!

I memorized it, and two days later, I was up in the Ménilmontant area of Paris, doing my new shtick to an older French crowd. They laughed at every joke, and at every line of the song. I was a smash hit.

I decided that Stephen was now going to be my writer.

We started working together, and I began to be a hit in all the French clubs in Paris. I performed four times at France's most prestigious comedy venue, The Jamel Comedy Club.

* * *

THEN ONE DAY IN THE spring of 2018, I got a call from a producer inviting me to perform in a nightclub in Montparnasse, as an audition for the TV show, *France Incroyable Talent* (the French version of *America's Got Talent*). They were selecting candidates for the next season, which was to be filmed in the fall. This was potentially my big break.

The club was packed with about a hundred people ranging from the ages of 8 to 80, and I did a six-minute slot of my best French material, including my cougar song. And I was a smash. Even the kids loved me. So, I was invited to attend the second round of auditions in August, which would be filmed in front of a huge audience. The producers said if I got voted through by three members of a four-person celebrity jury, my act would be broadcast on their TV show in the fall. Of course, I said, "Formidable!"

My spirit was more than willing, but it turned out that my flesh was weak.

I went back to the States in the early summer, and somehow a disk in my upper back collapsed. I was on heavy painkillers and could hardly move. I told my doctor that I needed to be on my feet again to do a TV show in Paris in August, and he said it was very unlikely.

"Can't you do the show in a wheelchair?" he asked me. "And from New York?"

"This is my big break in Europe," I told him.

"But you don't want it to break your back."

I was determined to be on that stage in front of that jury, so I took my X-rays to a surgeon, who agreed to operate. He pumped cement into the affected vertebra. I felt a bit like an old building getting its foundations reinforced, to stop it keeling over. The operation didn't decrease the pain all that much but at least I could stand up, and as soon as I was given medical clearance, I was on a plane to Paris.

I got there just three days before the audition, and only had time for a couple of rehearsals before I was due to perform in French, in front of 600 people—in agony.

Stephen and my assistant, Rob Winston, accompanied me for the big event in a huge TV auditorium just outside of Paris.

The production was a well-oiled machine. When we arrived at the theater, there were dozens of acts lining up to get badges: a big group of excited teenage girls from Marseille practicing their dance moves, a singer warming up his voice, an acrobat doing scary back bends that made me wince. It was as if the performance was beginning even before we got on stage.

We got in line (a painful business for me, just having to stand for twenty minutes), I received my performers' badge, and I had to sign a lot of papers that I really didn't have time to read. (When I read them next day, I realized I had signed away all my TV rights to the material in the show. Too bad that we contestants didn't have a chance to read the contract a few days before! But that's showbiz.)

A photographer had set up a small studio, and the performers had to get into costume then line up again (ouch!) to wait for our turn to pose. The photographer took about 200 shots of me in my sparkly silver jacket, with my Eiffel Tower hat and my ukulele.

Then we were sent to an enormous backstage waiting room where there were about 100 performers, including the 30 girls who were going to do a dance routine. The room was lined with mirrors and three or four teams of rushed make-up artists were making sure that we all had enough pancake on our faces to avoid looking shiny on camera.

There was an overdose of adrenaline in the air. I was feeling a little drowsy because of my painkillers, but I just had to take a deep breath and I was high. All the acts, including a juggler and the dancing girls, were rehearsing in between the couches that half-filled the waiting room. It was a noisy chaos of shrill voices and flying limbs, with a photographer's flashlight popping non-stop, and a camera crew filming the backstage excitement.

It was four in the afternoon and I was told I wouldn't go on until nine. Fine, I thought, time to take a couple of painkillers, put in some earplugs and have a nap on the couch they'd assigned me to.

No such luck. They had me film four different interviews in French, including some painfully forced conversations with other contestants. One of them was a woman disguised as half-man, half horse. What kind of conversation could I have with her: "Bonjour, exactly how confused are you about your identity?"

Some of the girl dancers asked me, "how old are you?" (Well, it was one of the producers who told them to ask.)

"Quatre-vingt-quatre," I told them (that's 84 in French).

"How old!?" They couldn't believe it.

"That's as old as one of my great-grandmothers," a girl told me.

"Merci beaucoup," I said. I was feeling more like 184.

"Excellent!" the TV crew said. "Now can you have the same conversation while we film you from a different angle?"

"Sure," I said, "just let me go and get another painkiller."

Around 6 pm, I started to get really hungry, but the only food on offer was baskets of bananas and apples, a big box of children's candy, and flasks of coffee. Where was France's famous gastronomy?

I lay down and closed my eyes but with 30 over-excited teenagers in the room, there was no chance of getting any rest. In any case, I was constantly being told, "Come and do some more photos," "Come and say hello to a contortionist," "The horse-man-lady has to talk to you again."

Finally, about 7 pm, I was asked to go on stage for a dress rehearsal in front of the production team. They took my ukulele away from me because they wanted to fit a microphone on it. I had to do my shtick without an audience, and without a ukulele, but the producer said it was fine.

"Just make sure you speak slowly and clearly," he said, "and try to get your French grammar correct." Grammar? I was more worried about dropping dead than getting my verb endings right.

Then it was back to the waiting room.

THE SHOW BEGAN REALLY LATE, and I was going on near the end, so it wasn't until 10 pm that I finally got my call.

I went down to the stage area, but it was only to film yet another interview. Then they gave me some lines that I would deliver when a handsome ex-football player (David Ginola, the show's host) introduced me. He was going to come on and bring me my ukulele.

As you can imagine, by the time I went on at 10:30 pm, I was starved (well, full of candy and bananas), exhausted and half-dead with the painkillers I'd been taking just to get through all the stuff they'd been making me do. It's really difficult to smile for the cameras when you're in agony.

On stage at last, in front of the crowd and the cameras, I felt much more alive. It was that good old showbiz buzz, as my body told me "the show must go on."

The celebrity jurors greeted me warmly, asked me questions, and I gave them my best French banter.

"Bonsoir, je suis Américaine et je suis cougar ..." I gave the audience a cat-like growl and got an immediate laugh.

I started performing, and the handsome footballer was supposed to wait until I said I would now sing a cougar song. But he screwed up, and came out as I was doing my second line. When I saw him coming, I thought "not now, you're going to ruin everything!", so I chased him away. And this got a huge laugh from the crowd. I realized that, either accidentally or deliberately, he'd loosened things up for me, and after that the 600-strong audience laughed at every line. Finally, the footballer brought my ukulele on at the right time, I sang my song, and I got a standing ovation. Things were feeling very good. I wasn't even in pain anymore.

Now it was time for the jury's verdict. I needed three votes out of the four to go through to the next round and get my big break on French TV.

The first juror was a guy, a stand-up comedian who was well known on the Paris comedy scene for not being particularly funny. He was one of those French stand-ups who just insults people to show how smart he is. A wise guy. Well, he did his wise-guy act on me. He said my material was not great, and gave me a "non". The audience booed him.

Damn, I thought, now I needed all three of the other judges' approval to go through. I began to sweat. My back was suddenly throbbing again.

The second judge, a female comedian, told the first guy he'd been a spoilsport.

"You were formidable," she told me, "oui!"

The third judge said he loved the way I'd kicked David Ginola off stage, and for that alone I deserved a "oui".

So it was all down to the final judge. This was another woman, and she started talking, and I heard the audience laughing, but I couldn't really understand what she was saying, or even hear it for that matter because my heart was thumping in my ears. I was just waiting to see if her spiel would finish with a glorious "oui" or a disastrous "non."

She kept talking, making wisecracks, milking the laughter, and I thought, "come on, I'm going to have a heart attack in a minute," and then suddenly she said "oui!" and the audience were on their feet and cheering, and I waved goodbye and came off stage in a cloud of painkillers and pure happiness.

THE DAY'S WORK WASN'T OVER yet, of course. In the wings, yet another film crew interviewed me, and then when I got backstage, one of the presenters had me sing a duet of "New York, New York" with him, while they filmed us. He didn't know the words, but I was past caring.

After all that, an executive from Sony took me to a private room and asked me to sign a contract for their production company to represent me during the live tour of the show, after the televised version had been aired. All the acts were going to perform in major theaters around France. Of course, I said "oui"!

By now, I didn't need the painkillers anymore. I had my three votes, and they took away all the pain of the previous weeks. My big TV break was just around the corner. I was already high as a kite, but the only way was up even higher.

OVER THE NEXT MONTH THE producers kept emailing me. They asked if I had more material for the show in October—of course I did. I was already writing it with Stephen.

Then they filmed me walking around Paris, talking about my favorite parts of the city. I took them to the *bouquinistes'* stalls by the Seine, and told the interviewer this was where I used to buy risqué books when I first came to Paris. They were very happy with the footage we shot, and told me it was for a background segment about each candidate that would be broadcast just before our act was shown. I was ready to be famous!

Then, at the beginning of October, one of the producers left me a telephone message.

"Bonjour, D'yan, this is just to tell you you're not going to be on the show. "

I couldn't believe it. I had to listen to the voicemail again. But it was true—I'd been axed. I didn't get it. Had I dreamed my standing ovation and my three votes from the jury?

I called back, and got through to one of the producers who had been telling me for weeks that I was great and would be a big hit when the show was broadcast.

"I don't understand," I told her. "Why have I been cut?"

"There's just not room for you. Too many performers got the three votes."

"Did they all get standing ovations like I did?"

"No, but this is what's been decided. Sorry, D'yan."

And that was it. I was heartbroken. My big break in France was not to be.

Of course, when the first show of the new season was broadcast, I had to watch it. Cruelly, my photo was used in the opening titles. And then once the acts began to perform, I understood why I'd been ousted. There was only one non-French person on the show, a Chinese dancer who, before she performed, gave an impassioned speech about how lucky she was to be in France, because back home she didn't have any artistic freedom (so you can't dance in China? Really?), and "merci beaucoup for giving me this opportunity" and "vive la France," and the whole flatter-the-French, milk-the-audience shtick. She cried, the audience cried, the jury wept, and one of the jurors came on stage to hug her.

The penny dropped. The producers of the show didn't want *talent*. They wanted *TV*.

I realized that maybe when I went out on stage, I should have shown them my X-rays and my prescription for painkillers, perhaps even a video of my operation. That would have brought tears to their eyes, as it had done to mine.

I understood that I'd got it all wrong. Sticking to my philosophy of "the show must go on," gritting my teeth and hiding the agony had been counter-productive. These days, you have to share your pain, you have to cry, you have to emote.

Well, sorry, but I just *perform*.

Anyway, there was no point crying over spilt *lait*.

I told Stephen I wanted to put together an entirely new one-hour act, in English, and we sat down and wrote a show that Stephen called *Swinging on the Seine*.

It's the story of my whole voyage of self-discovery from innocent Bostonian to Parisian swinger, focusing on my wild adventures in Paris in the swinging sixties, after my divorce.

The theme song is a comedy version of "Singing in the Rain" and it describes the swinger's parties I used to go to: "I'm lying on a bed without any clothes/Fifty French asses right under my nose."

Then there are the stories about my first Parisian (Austrian) boyfriend, my first strip club, and how I started performing with transvestites in a Montparnasse cabaret—all punctuated with snippets of song that I accompany on the ukulele or the piano.

I've performed the show in Paris and in New York, and it goes down really well in both cities. It's provocative, but it's playful, and people tell me they can't believe I really did all this sexy stuff. The fact that it all happened 50 or 60 years ago, and in Paris, makes it seem more glamorous and romantic to them. Which it was—the world was a much less cynical place back then. After seeing *Swinging on the Seine*, the older American ladies come up to me and say, "oh, I wish I'd been to Paris and done all that!"

But more than the sex, the show is about my own evolution, about how I gradually found out who I am, and realized that in Paris, I found acceptance. It's a city of misfits, so I fit right in. Sure, the kids in a French comedy basement think it's weird when, between two bearded hipsters boasting about their drug intake, an old lady gets up on stage to talk about her 60-year-long love life, but the young crowds laugh with me and seem to admire me for being so frank. They certainly don't judge me.

That's the freedom I get in Paris—no judgement. There's snobbery amongst Parisians, for sure, but it's mainly confined to a few select restaurants and dinner parties. I can go into almost any café in Paris, and no one cares that I'm an aging bisexual Jewish American. That's why to me, Paris represents true liberty, and every time I go there, the city shows me what I love about life.

And as I've said, thanks to all my showbiz experience—the singing, the piano-playing, the comedy, and combining them all in my one-woman shows—I've realized that my greatest love of all is performing. I don't give a damn about age, I want to get up on stage.

I've decided that from now on, I'm going to do a show at every birthday. Sadly, I missed out on my 86th because of that bitch Covid-19. But I'm already looking forward to my 87th. And so what if people don't believe me when I get up on stage and tell them I'm performing at 87? How will they react when I'm 88, 89, 90, 100?

Something tells me I might have to bring along my birth certificate.

Epilogue

To sum up my life in two events, I have to go back in time.

First, to my first experience as a girl who suddenly realized she was a woman. I was about 15 years old, had just finished summer camp in New Hampshire, and while my parents were playing golf, I was walking along the road when a car drove by and the driver whistled at me. Wow!

I had only seen this in the movies, and now here was someone whistling at me. Nowadays whistling is frowned upon as sexual harassment. Well, this may be an example of how my way of thinking doesn't fit in, but as far as I'm concerned, each individual can take it the way they want, and back then the whistle made me realize that I was attractive enough to interest a man, and that this was probably the beginning of the grown-up phase of my life.

I, of course, thought the whistling would last forever. Sadly, that is not true. As you know from reading my story, I've had plenty of lovers and relationships, with both men and women. I've had a lot of fun. However, in the last few years, it's changed. My brain is just the same, my personality hasn't changed, and my vibrancy is just as great as, or greater than, many friends my age. Hell, I even have a brand-new vertebra and cleaned-out arteries.

The problem for me is that, as an older lady, from a sexual point of view I am dismissed or ignored when I walk into a room. It can be a bar, a party or even a comedy club. I am looked at as just another old lady who has nothing to titillate. My older friends all say the same thing—they feel invisible. It's a tough truth to face. If you're like me, you feel as much desire as you ever did (well, almost), but no one really wants to know. In these days of so-called tolerance, when it's supposedly OK to be gay, bi, or a hundred different combinations, an old lady's desire is the love that dare not speak its name. Or the love that isn't listened to.

WHICH BRINGS ME TO THE second event. It happened in 2011, when I came to Paris and—foolishly perhaps—tried to relive the excitement of my younger days in the city of lights and love.

It really taught me a lesson.

It was New Year's Eve. I was staying with friends but decided to go out on the town. I mean, really go to town.

I was just off the Champs-Élysées and found exactly what I wanted: a place called the Club Cheminée. A plaque outside said, "women admitted at half-price." My kind of place.

Inside, the sweetest girl said, "Bonsoir, Madame" and took my coat. The bartender reached over and gave me a big hug, "Welcome, Madame." I'd never set foot in the place before, but it was like old home week.

A Swedish guy, a tourist in from Sweden, swept over and introduced himself.

"Bonsoir, I'm Gustav, let me give you a guided tour."

"Merci, I'm D'yan, let's go, Gustav."

First, he took me into the dining room—red carpets and chandeliers, and on the buffet table, smoked salmon and shrimp, ham, melon, and all the champagne you could drink.

"Santé!" Gustav and I clinked glasses and enjoyed a cheery sip of champagne.

Next, he took my arm and led me down a steeply winding staircase to the lower floor. As we stepped into a dimly lit hallway, he said, "You realize this is a swinger's club?"

I laughed. "Oh, yes, yes, fifty years ago, I went wild at one very much like this."

"Très bien," he said, and reached around me to open a door. I looked into a room that was furnished with several long, wide, black couches. I knew exactly what went on there. It both thrilled me and terrified me as I thought about the long night ahead. Just because you crossed a threshold once in your life, it doesn't mean you can cross it again.

In the center of the room was a floor-to-ceiling pole. It was inviting. Not that I was going to gyrate around it myself, but I did want to touch it, and lean against it. I shuddered with nervous anticipation. Fifty years after she lost her innocence in a place just like this, the shy girl from Boston was back.

"There is more," Gustav said, pulling me away from the pole and taking me out into the corridor.

He opened another door, and this room really took my breath away. It was filled almost entirely with a huge padded table.

"This is the *bang-bang* room," Gustav said, "where women ... *bang-bang!*" My mouth dropped open. "You see, chérie," he went on, "this is for a woman who likes to have one *bang* after another *bang*. She stretches out, she spreads her legs, and..."

I could guess: "Bang-bang-bang?"

"Exactly. We enjoy them, they enjoy us!"

My hair stood on end. This wasn't my refined, sophisticated Paris of 50 years ago, where there was some semblance of innocence—a teasing glance, a titillating touch before the "fun" began, in a crowd but usually one or two on one. There was no *bang-bang* room. Well, not in a chic place like this.

Gustav could see that I was horrified. He took my arm and led me gently along the hall to yet another room.

"Here," he said, "this is the room for a woman like you."

But I didn't even look inside, I just couldn't. I had no idea what was in there: a hot tub, a massage table, a therapist's chair? I didn't want to know.

I said, "Merci, merci, let's go back upstairs!" I was going to cut and run.

But when we returned to the dining room, the smell of food and wine caught me. So did the short dresses on many of the women who'd arrived, their split skirts revealing some intriguing curves. I dipped my glass in the punch bowl, a time or three, and felt better.

There were attractive couples and single men, chatting in French, which I've always found to be the most seductive, civilized language in the world. It's something about the way the mouth puckers forward as they speak. Hey, I thought, what harm could there be drinking, eating, relaxing with these people till midnight? Who wants to be alone on New Year's Eve?

Two fellows from Luxembourg chatted with me while we ate. But as soon as they finished dinner, they were off downstairs in a flash. The same thing happened with a French couple. As soon as they'd drained their coffee, they stopped talking and dashed for the stairs. I looked around and saw that *everyone* had disappeared.

So, I, too, lit by wine, went downstairs. Maybe I was hoping that I could open a door back to the frolicking days of my youth. But peering into the *bang-bang* room, I saw how wrong I was. It was packed. Stretched out on the padded table, a woman, her clothes tossed to the side, was enjoying several men. They were all over her. Gone were the old-fashioned days of mischievous foreplay! Several of the men surrounding the table couldn't bear to wait their turn: they took "themselves in hand," right then and there.

I was speechless! This wasn't sweet swinging. This was gang-banging. Where's the beauty in that? Someone told me that the elegant man in a tux, ogling this orgy, was the woman's husband. Very Parisian, you might think, the city where anything goes. But it was a lot more than I could handle. This time, I was definitely out of there.

But first, heady from the fruit punch, dizzy from the sight of the bang-bang room, I had to go sit down. Where was that room with the long couches?

I found it, flung myself down on a long settee, and within seconds, like flies to honey, guys were swarming around me. With nary a *bonsoir*, they were unzipped and ready to go.

But that just isn't my style. I wanted to swing, sure, but this girl needs a little warm-up. Where was the conversation, the flirtation? If only for a few minutes? *Please!* I brushed off one. I brushed off another. They didn't care. With polite *adieux*, they went off in search of greener pastures. I was ready to cry.

Finally, wonder of wonders, a fellow about my age sat down beside me. He had all the prelims down. Where was

I from? How did I find the place? What did I love about Paris? He told me he was Turkish, and he was charming, and good to talk to.

I relaxed, and we had our "fun," or at least I had mine while staying completely dressed in my woolen slacks and sweater. I gave thanks to God for giving men nimble hands and adroit fingers.

I had no idea what was going on in his trousers, because I kept my hands to myself. In the room around us, all the men were unzipped, and flagpoles were flying high. I've never seen so many waggling poles in my lifetime! But this Turkish fellow, the whole time, kept his private things private. A girl from Boston appreciates such decorum, so now I was settled in and ready. Ready for something a little more daring perhaps. But then he rushed off and left me alone!

Embarrassed in ways I can't explain—I mean, hadn't I had some fun? —I went back upstairs to the bar to drink something stronger than punch. I wondered if I could catch a woman's eye. I thought that a woman might be more into subtlety and sophistication. But no woman in the room would even talk to me! They were totally straight, here for the guys. They were into doing daring stuff, but strictly along conventional lines.

One of the guys I'd seen earlier in the *bang-bang* room came upstairs for a drink, and he explained it all.

"This," he said, "is a club where women come especially for the *bang-bang*, where men come especially for the *bang-bang*, but where men definitely *don't* come for other men or women for other women."

"Just hetero-bang-bang?" I asked.

"Exactement."

"Things really have changed," I told him.

Fifty years ago in the Parisian swingers' clubs, *any* combination of men and women would do. But now, at the Cheminée, there were boundaries you didn't cross: "anything goes" was just a pose.

One by one, everyone in the bar trailed back downstairs. I was left sitting alone, until one very young fellow came over and sat down beside me. Judging by his accent, he was French.

"When you came in," he told me, "I noticed your sparkling, smiling, blue eyes, and I had to get to know you." Well, those were the right words to pick up a girl's spirits.

"Merci," I told him, "you've made the evening feel much more civilized."

"To be totally civilized, we need more champagne," he said, and went to get us a couple of glasses.

What a well brought-up young man, I thought, an excellent advertisement for the French education system.

An even better advertisement was the kiss he gave me, accompanied by plenty of compliments and gently caressing hands.

This time, feeling more at ease, I got more playful and reached on over. We *both* had some fun.

But then, just like all the others, once he'd got what he wanted, he rushed off. It was awful. Love was a vanishing act in this place!

But then, I told myself, this was sex, not love. I was getting much too philosophical about it. What did I expect from these party people—an invitation to their country house? A long-term relationship? No, they were all here to see in the New Year with a bang. Or a bang-bang. I just had to accept that this was what I'd let myself in for.

I hung around, thinking at least I'd stay until midnight, to toast the New Year with some champagne and (hopefully) some more company.

Then the young fellow came back into the bar and strolled over.

"How old are you *exactly*?" he asked me. I was offended.

"I thought you were well-bred," I told him, "but you've already forgotten how to talk to a lady."

"I'm sorry. I'm 39, and I was just wondering how old you were because I think you are very vivacious for your age." That was more like it.

"I'm very old," I told him, "too old for all of this."

He shook his head. "Non," he said. "L'amour n'a pas d'âge." Love has no age.

I'd never heard this before. I thought, love has no age, what a beautiful phrase.

I hated him, of course, for trying out a stupid line like that on me. It was too smooth to be real. But then tears came to my sparkling, supposedly smiling, blue eyes. He really meant it.

"In Paris," he said, "as long as you are charming and willing to play along, men and women don't care how old you are."

Which was very reassuring, but it didn't stop him dashing off downstairs again for some more action.

MIDNIGHT ARRIVED AND SEVERAL GUYS came over and gave me strangely innocent New Year's kisses. And then they hurried off again, this time, out the door into the street. They were going to catch the subway—back then, the Paris Métro stopped at 1 am. If you wanted to get home, you had to dash!

I caught a taxi and made my way home. Everyone was out in the streets: tourists and French families, young lovers and old, roaming around in couples and groups, laughing, singing, drinking, or just enjoying the communal feeling of celebration. As my taxi crossed the Seine, I saw the Eiffel Tower flickering with 10,000 lights. It was magical. I wanted to get out and join the crowds, but I was exhausted from my excursion to the club. And I was alone.

And then it hit me. Love has no age? What bullshit! Of *course,* love has an age. Otherwise that young guy might have stayed with me for longer instead of heading downstairs to check out the action with the spring chickens.

And when I went to another swinger's club just after that, a place where I used to go 50 years earlier, they opened the little peephole in the door, looked me over, and wouldn't even let me in!

"Sorry, Madame, no single ladies tonight."

What bullshit! Those places want as many single women as they can get. A woman on her own is gold dust in a swingers' club. But I was left out in the street, and just because of my wrinkles.

TODAY, THIS FEELING OF BEING trapped by my age goes almost everywhere with me.

Just imagine that you're a comedian, and you go backstage before a show to hang out with the other comics, who are much younger, and they ignore you. They talk amongst themselves. It's pretty insulting, but it's often true. There might be one or two who are friendly and interested, but on the whole they're indifferent. Even the MCs won't listen to how I want to be introduced until 30 seconds before I walk on stage. Seems I'm not hip enough for them to care.

Of course, as soon as I'm out on stage, I'm as visible as you can get. Once I start telling my stories and singing my songs, people realize that I've got a hell of a lot to contribute, that I really can titillate. Occasionally, young comedians hear me getting laughs and come out of the backstage area to see what's going on.

And after a show, both in France and in the States, young people from the audience come over and tell me I'm an inspiration. They say they hope they will be as vibrant as I am when they're in their 80s. It's a huge compliment.

And after my spot, the other comics and the MC are usually very friendly and complimentary. They've seen that I can handle myself on stage, that I know how to work a crowd, that I have professional material, so suddenly I amount to something. I'm a little old lady, but with a sting in the tail.

What I mean is, in comedy clubs and theaters, I get the chance to win people over. I'm on stage, so they sit back and listen to me.

I just wish it was the same in my personal life.

I've been single for five years now. It's partly because I'm getting picky after my disappointing relationships. But it's also because at my age, I don't get hit on very often these days.

So yes, I'm single. But isn't that great news for all you readers!?

That's one of the reasons why I wrote this book. Maybe there's somebody out there who would be interested in getting to know the *real* D'yan, not just from seeing me cracking jokes or singing songs on stage. Now you know *everything*. I've told you the tragic stories as well as all the funny stuff.

So if anyone wants to get in touch, check me out on Facebook. You just have to be fun, intelligent and titillating. Like I said, I'm very picky these days.

But I don't care how old you are. For me, love really does have no age.

Just let me know: who wants to do it my ways?

Acknowledgements

D'yan Forest would like to thank:

Stephen Clarke who made my dream come true to help me write this book.

Andrea Alton, my best buddy and New York City publicist.

Rob Winston, my Parisian friend and publicist for helping me in France.

Natacha Henry for the encouragement.

Carlos, Anne and Pascal Otero who for the last 40 years have given me a Parisian place to stay and have been my Paris family.

Andy Engel, my New York City comedy mentor and friend, for booking me (for more than 10 years) on his shows at Gotham Comedy Club in NYC.

Eric Kornfeld, who listened to all my stories and helped me incorporate them into my one-woman shows.

Lucille DeSimone, a golf friend of 30 years, who reminded me of all my different identities. I sent her my book by mistake and she read it in eight hours and provided lots of encouragement.

Jenny Hughes, who published my first stories in *Frenchly* magazine.

Lily Phillips, my London comedian friend, who has been instrumental in helping me along by reading my stories and giving feedback.

Georgia Clark & Lindsay Ratowsky of Generation Women for pointing me in the right direction for publishing and publicity.

Sarah Cypher for all her editing help and feedback.

Caroline Hirsch, golf friend and owner of Carolines On Broadway comedy club in New York City, who helped get me started.

Felicia Sobel and Brooke Fisher, my New York and Paris friends respectively, for always coming to my shows and giving their opinion.

And my parents, Dorothy Lunn & Louis Shulman, who did the best they could with an outlier like me.

Also, in no special order, but sincere thanks to: Gotham Comedy Club, Don't Tell Mama Comedy Club, The Duplex, Joe's Pub, Roger Paul Management, Berklee School of Music, Middlebury College, Stephen Jobes, Rabbi Joyce Renitz, Rabbi Ira Schiffer, and the ever-present Mira Grodska and Bogdan Grodski.

Stephen Clarke would like to thank N, L, S, and the Friday lunch club for being there, as well as everyone who has come along to see the stage show *Swinging on the Seine*; Valli Budestschu and Katrin Hodapp who made some *très* useful comments on the manuscript; and most of all D'yan, for telling me all her secrets, for bringing so many of my one-liners and song words to life in theaters, and for letting me come on stage and share a few of the laughs. Also for showing me what a *real* performer is: it doesn't matter if you feel tired, old, discouraged or about to drop dead, you get up on stage and go for it. Pure positive energy, it's inspiring.